Praise for *Seeing in the Dark*

"The kind of book that offers newcomers to shamanism a safe and sensible program and also reminds experienced practitioners why they fell in love with shamanism in the first place. The authors carefully guide readers through the many aspects of the shamanic life and offer practical suggestions for journeys, ceremonies, and personal healing. This book will become a comforting and reliable companion for those on the shaman's path."

—Tom Cowan, author of *Shamanism: A Spiritual Practice for Daily Life* and *Fire in the Head*

"A groundbreaking work of startling authenticity. This book is a necessity for those who wish to understand how personal reality can be shaped by one's beliefs and how the fate of individuals and nations can be shifted by the focused intent of inwardly directed individuals. *Seeing in the Dark* is ideal for those seeking a practical application of material garnered from readings in comparative religious studies, folklore, and mythology but were left looking for the next step—here it is. Take it if you dare."

—Mark Stavish, Director of Studies, Institute for Hermetic Studies and author of *Between the Gates*

"Shamanism is many things to many people—at its core it is an ancient spiritual tradition dedicated to becoming fully human. Through partnership with the compassionate spirits, shamanic practitioners bring blessings of balance and healing to our world. In *Seeing in the Dark*, Colleen and Paul offer us their inspired, multi-faceted perspective, helping to make this powerful tradition more readily available at a time when our need for it has never been greater."

—Nan Moss and David Corbin, authors of *Weather Shamanism*

"*Seeing in the Dark* is a wonderful gateway to shamanic practice. Packed with wonderful exercises and journey suggestions, it gently guides readers to find insight and healing through spirit connections and energy work."

—Kristin Madden, author of *Magick, Mystery, and Medicine; The Book of Shamanic Healing;* and *Shamanic Guide to Death and Dying*

"*Seeing in the Dark* is both a step-by-step guide to developing powerful kinships with the spirits who surround us and to nurturing a clearer understanding of our place in the Universe."

—Evelyn C. Rysdyk, Shamanic teacher and healer, author of *Modern Shamanic Living*

"The world of the soul often seems too mystical for us to travel, and yet we know the mysteries are there, hidden just beyond our view. Colleen Deatsman and Paul Bowersox dispel those myths, teaching students how to begin and then guiding the experienced practitioner on ways to continue. Every reader will deepen their understanding of their own soul and the spiritual worlds of mystery."

—Gail Wood, co-author of *Shamanic Witch* and author of *Sisters of the Dark Moon*

"Colleen Deatsman and Paul Bowersox draw on their diverse spiritual training and personal experience to craft a book that gives readers tools with which to traverse the turmoils of everyday life, economic downturns, and personal struggles. This is the sort of 'engaged shamanism' that can light up the dark."

—Larry G. Peters, Ph.D., anthropologist, licensed psychotherapist, and author of *The Yeti*

Seeing in the Dark

Claim Your Own Shamanic Power
Now and in the Coming Age

Colleen Deatsman and Paul Bowersox

WEISER BOOKS
San Francisco, CA/Newburyport, MA

To our parents
LaVon and Donna Deatsman
and Don and Marilee Bowersox

First published in 2009 by
Red Wheel/Weiser, LLC
With offices at:
500 Third Street, Suite 230
San Francisco, CA 94107
www.redwheelweiser.com

ISBN: 978-1-57863-443-9
Library of Congress Cataloging-in-Publication Data available upon request.

Cover and interior design by Maija Tollefson
Typeset in Cochin
Cover photograph © Elena Ray

Printed in Canada
TCP
10 9 8 7 6 5 4 3 2 1

Contents

Acknowledgments

Colleen offers special thanks to:

Pat, Lauren, Laura, and Erin—for supporting my dreams; the Helping Spirits who orchestrated and directed this journey; my phenomenal shaman friends—participants, students, and teachers of hundreds of circles over many years;

Judy, my dearly beloved wise-woman mentor, colleague, and soul-comrade;

Sandra Ingerman, Tom Cowan, Larry Peters, Myron Eshowsky, Michael Harner, Nan Moss, David Corbin, Patrick Jasper Lee, Judy, and John Worthington for keeping shamanism alive;

Stephanie and Kate of Spiritweavers for bringing shamanism to Michigan;

Caroline Pincus, executive editor for Red Wheel/Weiser Books and Conari Press, whose vision made this book a reality.

Paul especially thanks:

My brother Bob and sister Maggie, as well as Ken, Kate, Zach, and Taylor, for lovingly indulging my eccentricities all these years;

soul sisters Toni and Stephanie, for loving me no matter what;

Aunt Jeanne, for being the best of us;

Pat Kelley, for helping make this reality work as well as it does;

my friends at *www.TheOtherForum.net*, for working to make a difference;

Michael Harner, for bringing shamanism home;

John Worthington, for filling in the missing pieces.

Introduction

The world is changing.

Environmentally, we are seeing increases in the frequency and magnitude of storms. Earthquakes are prevalent and devastating worldwide. The ice caps are melting, ocean levels are rising, and more arable land each year either disappears or becomes barren.

Sociologically and culturally, we are seeing an increase in extremes and a shrinking of the middle. Wealth is concentrating in the hands of the very few, and poverty is increasing among the masses. We are experiencing a social divide in opportunity, which further stratifies the division between the haves and have-nots.

Technologically, we have automated ourselves to the point where very few know how to manufacture or produce the vast majority of what we consume. It is significant that we have a new generation of computer technology every three months, while most of us would be stymied should we be required to manufacture a paper clip from raw materials. We don't understand our own technology.

We have also become a species who has lost its inclination for self-determination. We allow ourselves to be told how to act, what to do, what to want, and even who or what to love. The mainstream religious practices are fundamentally exclusive, rather than inclusive — that is, they posit an idea that if you do not believe as they do, your soul will be denied reward of any kind, because theirs is the only way.

In essence we are a tribal species who have just enough out-of-control technology and little enough wisdom so that we are capable of doing some real damage.

And we are.

So, in the midst of devastating change, what can we do? Well, if the world trend is to isolate and become more dependent on a tenuous infrastructure, and that's not working, perhaps we should consider an alternate point of view. Maybe the answer is to become more connected, more self-reliant, and unswervingly responsible for ourselves.

What kind of paradigm, model, or philosophy can provide that? If everything changes, where can we look to find an immutable constant that has weathered the ravages of time?

The answer to that question is shamanism. It has even survived evolution.

In 1972, two French archeologists unearthed a 50,000-year-old Neanderthal burial site in Southern France. At this site, called the Hortus site, they found the body of a man wearing a leopard hide, complete with claws and tail. There were no other leopard bones in the grave. The only cultural comparison we can see in the archeological or anthropological record is that tribal shamans in certain cultures are known to wear animal capes in their rituals. They are buried with these magical garments. It is widely accepted among scientists that the Neanderthal man found at the Hortus site was a shaman.

This and other evidence demonstrates that shamanism has been around since before people were even people. It outlived the Neanderthal and has flourished for tens of thousands of years to the present day. If it has been able to survive that long, it must have something of value to offer those who practice it. Certainly, if shamanism can endure through all the changes of the last 50,000 years and even the death of an entire species, it can help us during these times of change.

The reason shamanism is so effective is that it is a point of view, a lifestyle, rather than a doctrine. It is experiential in nature and teaches us that we know, on a very fundamental level, who we are and what we need to do to take care of ourselves. It provides a way of self-examination and natural connection that can help us find our way, even when we are lost or confused. It is possible to believe anything you want to believe and still be a shaman. You can embrace any god, prophet, or savior you desire, and shamanism will still work for you. Why? Because shamanism teaches us how to live in harmony with all of creation. Its overarching tenet is that we are all connected, and because of this connection, we can rely on ourselves to fulfill our destinies. More than that, we can use the principles of shamanism to do the personal work that will ultimately allow us to choose an alternate course for this world.

Hindu scholars say we are at the lowest point of the darkest age of a repeating cycle that began 12,800 years ago, when our summer-solstice sun aligned with the galactic center of the Milky Way galaxy. They claim we will begin our ascent back to light when the winter-solstice sun aligns with the galactic center in 2012. Coincidentally, this date is when the famed Mayan calendar ends and when several of the most prominent modern alchemists in America and France believe the dimensional door will shut, leaving only those on the planet who will continue their spiritual evolution back to the transcendent light.

All of this speculation is nothing more than an abstraction. What matters is if we can find a way to make a difference in our own lives and in the lives of others. Sitting alone in the dark, wringing our hands about what is coming, only helps to manifest that which we dread. The key to the coming age is to remain engaged, get out into the world, do substantive work to initiate change, and find those who can pick the necessary agreements to precipitate a new reality. That is the essence of shamanism.

Before we delve into the techniques associated with engaged sha-manism, it is important to think about what it means to be your own shaman. Becoming your own shaman entails embarking upon a power path of unveiling and cultivating the sacred and spiritual in your everyday life and in the modern environment and culture in which you currently live. To effectively utilize the practices of shamanism you do not have to move into the wilderness or desert, or don a leopard cape or a feathered headdress. You do not have to practice someone else's ceremonies and rituals or pray at their sacred sites. In fact, doing so is adamantly discouraged, unless a reputable person of that culture teaches and gives you permission to perform these practices or allows you to visit these places.

Modern shamanism is not a practice of taking or borrowing someone else's religion or spiritual beliefs, nor does it involve copying the ways of the Mexican nagual, the Lakota medicine woman, African dagara healer, or Peruvian shaman. There is no need to imitate. The practice of shamanism is intimately personal and unique to every individual practitioner. No places, cultures, or peoples own these universal energies or the practices that access them. Animism, the Web of Life, Spirit, and sacredness are omnipresent; they are everywhere, in everything, and belong to everyone. Your personal, homemade, Spirit-directed ceremony can be just as effective as a traditional cultural ceremony when practiced with heart, focus, energy, and right intention. To effectively practice shamanism in our culture and modern environment we need only wake up to our awareness of self, life-force energy, and Spirit; reap the rich experiences available to us right here, right now; and make a difference in the world around us.

The beauty of shamanism is that it is universal. The practices and principles can be and are being applied around the world in many diverse cultures. Though shamanic practitioners may choose to learn from teachers of different backgrounds, they must ultimately incorporate their learnings into their own personal practice in their own culture and environment. Shamanic practices are Spirit's gift to all people, not only the indigenous people that have bravely risked their lives to keep this powerful way of living alive. We are all benefactors of this Spirit gift.

Michael Harner, noted luminary and grandfather of the neo-shamanic movement, notes with great insight that no matter how far we may be removed from our ancestral roots, we are all indigenous people from one place or another on this earth. Shamanism isn't about doing what the native peoples do exactly like they do it. It is about connecting with Spirit and one's self using practices that help one follow a balanced personal path.

No matter what is on the way, no matter what changes, cataclysms, devastation, joy, or boredom we must face in the coming age, what happens is for us to determine. Our destiny and the destiny of the world and its inhabitants are in our hands. Jesus said, "The kingdom of God is within you" (Luke 17:21). Many people come to shamanism to experience this principle on a personal level, and the great contribution of shamanism is that it provides us the means to do just that.

Let's get started.

Opening Prayer

Morning Prayer to the Four Airts
*I give thanks that I have risen again today
and to the great Rising of Life Itself.*

*As the sun brightens up the sky and earth,
may my soul be bright with gratitude
for all the good things in my life.
May I be generous in sharing these with others.*

*I give thanks that I have risen again today
and to the great Rising of Life Itself.*

*As the trees, rivers, animals and everything sing their songs of life,
may my soul sing the song of my heart.
May I sing it gladly whether in joy or in sorrow,
and may it help me find humor and laughter in the day.*

*I give thanks that I have risen again today
and to the great Rising of Life Itself.*

*As the sun crosses the sky to where it will set in the west,
may my soul proceed on its journey through life.
May I keep the vision of my life ever before me and may I have
faith that my life has meaning.*

*I give thanks that I have risen again today
and to the great Rising of Life Itself.*

*As everything in nature strives to live and survive,
may my soul be strong in its struggles.
May I meet adversity with courage and hope.*

*I give thanks that I have risen again today
and to the great Rising of Life Itself.*

*As the earth spreads out from me to the horizon,
may my soul expand to embrace it. May I speak the truth of the land
and take responsibility for my life.*

—Written by Tom Cowan, based on a nineteenth-century prayer from the Scottish Highlands[i]

CHAPTER ONE

The Shamanic Path

Bare awareness: the place where our mind
falls silent with inner knowing.

—Colleen Deatsman

Shamans are students and practitioners of awareness. They study the natural world, observing the ebb and flow of energies as these energies pass from one form to another, from one being to the next. Shamans study the ritual of life, looking beyond and beneath the surface in order to see the driving mechanisms of the universe. The universe is layered, and shamans use their finely honed awareness to peel back these layers and see what lies underneath each one. On the surface, a shaman sees the sun rise, reach its peak, and set in the evening. The typical ritual we know as a day has its beginning, middle, and end, but the shaman knows, through observation of the next layer, that this day ritual is a cycle. It happens again and again and again. More than that, this day cycle is part of the larger, more complex annual cycle—another layer. That year cycle is also merely a part of the grand cycle of our sun as it moves through the cosmos, orbiting the galactic center over the course of 226 million years—yet another layer.

A study of these cycles provides useful information, but through shamanic discipline we can also develop an awareness of the universe's underlying nature. The shaman observes the consistency and utter simplicity of these cycles and begins to appreciate a natural pattern. The day is a circular cycle, as is the year; the horizon is a circle, the world itself a circle, and, through observation, it appears to the shaman that life itself is a circle. The shaman sees mankind as but a traveler on this disc of world as we move through the circle of our existence. Observing even more deeply, the shaman sees that we travelers are changing the nature of our world. We do not drive the wheel of time or the circle of life, but we do affect the very nature of our reality. The shaman seeks to understand the dynamic and the mechanism of that change.

There are many tools in the shamanic toolbox to accomplish this understanding. In this book we will investigate quite a few of these tools; but keep in mind that shamanism is a discipline requiring awareness and responsible application of that awareness. It provides tools not only to change the way we perceive reality, but also to change reality as well. The world stands at a precipice, and it has been brought here by the choices we, as a species, have made. We have collectively agreed to be in exactly the position we are in. That's a humbling thought. We have arrived at this juncture, this intersection of space and time and circumstance, largely by addressing what we are *not* and what we think we need to *have*, rather than what we *are* and what it is we *can be*. The truth is, we are a magnificent species, the flower of the universe, but we don't act like it. We act like clever animals, striving to make sure we are fed, safe, and comfortable. In this regard, we aren't that much more evolved than a groundhog. As long as we are in our own little holes, safe and sound, we don't need to pay attention to the rest of the world. No wonder the world is in trouble.

Shamanism cultivates a broader view than the involute perspective of self-gratification. It demonstrates, through experience, that we are part of something much grander, that we have a responsibility to express what we have the potential to become. In so doing, we shape reality and can therefore chart a different course for the planet, our species, and ourselves. Shamanism operates in the *now*. It requires that we engage in the moment. As a discipline, it provides the framework within which we can observe the universe as it is, dream a new one, and connect the dots to get us there. This requires an awareness of what is, and a commitment to be here and apply what we know *right now*.

To a certain extent, what *is* can be defined and catalogued by empirical science or deduced through myriad natural philosophies. So what makes shamans unique in their ability to observe or function within extreme, unusual, or even confounding mundane circumstances that the coming age may present? Why does shamanism have an advantage over other disciplines when it comes to survival, adaptation, or the shifting of reality?

The answer is that shamans learn to observe with all levels of being. By exploring and utilizing methods of observation other than merely the five senses, the shaman can discern the forces that drive not only the universe, but also the individual sentient beings that live within it. We initially explore the limits, potential, and function of each element of self—body, mind, emotions, and soul/spirit.

We apply these elements of self by allowing the soul to express cleanly and clearly through our bodies and into the world. The shamanic life demands that we express soul in this manner. This is quite simple, really, as the expression of soul is perfectly natural. It is the added complexities of those things that get in the way of that, most particularly our conditioning, behaviors, and personal history, that are unnatural. Once we have integrated the self and can express soul in this manner, we can bring about positive change anywhere and everywhere we can secure Agreement to do so.

The circular nature of life demands that the shaman accept the soul as eternal, even while the body is ephemeral. Just as energy cannot be created or destroyed, neither can the soul. But if the body is temporary and the soul eternal, then the soul must have a reason, an agenda, for occupying a human body. Shamans discern this agenda and use their bodies as instruments of communication between the soul/spirit realm and the world. In order to be a clear channel for this communication, shamans must do the challenging work of clearing away attachments, disadvantageous or self-sabotaging behaviors, unhealthy mindsets and energetic blockages, and intrusions in order to integrate the self. This integration of body, mind, emotion, and soul allows shamans to be "hollow bones," allowing Spirit to express itself clearly and cleanly through them.

The shamanic path utilizes everything available in the realm of body, mind, and soul in order to establish an extraordinary awareness of the universe. As such, it is a path of unflinching honesty, requiring us to see what we observe *as it is*, not just how we want it to be or as we think it should be. But the expanded awareness is far more than merely the observations gathered by mind alone.

The shamanic path is the path of the heart and the soul. It is a path of beauty, wholeness, sacred living, oneness and connectedness with all things and nonthings, awareness, mindfulness, respect, honor, and gratitude. It's a path of extraordinary moments when nature and Spirit speak more clearly than the racket of our mental chatter and we stop everything and take notice, listening and feeling the message. It is a path where the central focus of life is creating balance, harmony, impeccability, and wholeness. It is a path that requires integrity and honesty—with one's self and others. The shamanic path is a loving, healing path that invites all, yet it is also a truth-revealing path, turning away initiates not yet ready to face the awesome truth of reality. If you will continually accept the challenge (typically a daily choice), we invite you into the sacred circle of personal shamanic practitioners—a circle where healing, growth, change, and transformation are constants and where miracles happen.

•••

She stared into the open sky knowing that she could fly. But how? "How can I fly with this human body?" she thought.

"By becoming me," said Great-grandfather, who shape-shifted into Loon, and they took off into the blue. They flew for miles over towering pines and rolling mountains, swooping through the valleys and skimming the glistening lakes. Diving deep into the clear water, she became the silvery fish they sought for nourishment, and then headed upstream, driven by instinct. At just the right place, the very place that all of her ancestors had created and ended life, her experience as the salmon ended, and she slowly dissolved into the bottom of the river. In what seemed like minutes, but in ordinary reality would have taken millions of years, the essence that was once her, then loon, then fish, became sediment, soil, mineral, seed, seedling, majestic pine, petrified wood, stone, mountain, jagged stone, rounded river stone, small pebble consumed by Loon, mineral in Loon's bones, Loon, Great-grandfather, and her once more.

"Energy, is energy, is energy," Great-grandfather instructs with a chuckle and a sweeping gnarled old hand. "The same energy that is you is me, the loon, the tree, the lake, the sky. The form that things take is determined by the density, compilation, and characteristics that the energy takes on at any given time. As you see, energy can be changed—we can change. We can change form to learn new things and have different experiences. We can change energy to heal imbalances. Misfortune, disease, and unhappiness are energies that can be changed into abundance, health, and joy. If you want to change something, intend for it to change. Use your mind and willpower to concentrate your energy, the energy of creation, and the energy of that thing. Focus the energy into the change. See it, feel it, experience it, and believe in the change. It's far easier than you think. Look, you just did it without thinking! Spirit will help if you ask. Trust and believe. It's as simple as converting an electric current into light, a kernel of corn into an ear of corn."

The path of shamanism will shape you in much the same way that energy shapes things in nature. The natural forces of destruction and creation will help you eliminate the things in your self and your life that no longer serve your highest good and cultivate those things that do. This transformative process will be unique to each person. For some, it will bring about a softening of the hard edges of the self and the ego, causing the mind and soul to become smooth like a river stone. For some, the process will facilitate them becoming more assertive and to stand solid and strong like a mountain. For some, the path will help them become firmly grounded and rooted in Mother Earth while they bend and sway with the winds of life, like the great trees. For some, the process will help them flow through life like the great rivers, liberating resistance and attachment in order to plummet into the abyss like the majestic waterfall. For all, the process is always experiential and pragmatic. This path requires more than studying, thinking, or knowing. The power of this path is doing, practicing, living, and being.

As we said in the introduction, shamanism is the oldest living path of spirituality and healing known to man. Shamanism is a way of life and a practice that is rich in tradition, eclecticism, and mysticism; as such, it is a living power path. It is currently practiced in many countries, where it coexists, blends with, and complements all the major and minor world religions, including Christianity, Buddhism, and Hinduism. It is practical, not dogmatic, largely non-dualistic, and has no specific set of rules to follow. Shamanism is interactive, creative, and constantly dynamic, based on what works in each unique set of circumstances.

The term *shaman* (pronounced *shah*-maan) has been adapted from the Tungus people of Siberia and means "one who sees in the dark."[ii] This name denotes the shamans' ability to journey out of ordinary space and time into nonordinary reality, where they connect with helping spirits to receive guidance, to gain insight or power, or to diagnose and treat illness. The term *seer* also reflects this ability to journey into nonordinary reality and experience extraordinary information firsthand. The shaman is the bridge between the ordinary reality in which we live and the nonordinary reality that exists just outside of our everyday perceptions.

The role of the shaman is diverse. Shamans are the counselors, advisors, mediators, and psychologists of their communities. They are the teachers of spiritual ways and the wise sages that understand the universal laws of energy and nature and know how to harness these energies for the benefit of the people. They are the doctors, nurses, midwives, bone-setters, herbalists, massage therapists, and the energy practitioners of their communities. In shamanism, physical, mental, and emotional illnesses are recognized as being caused by spiritual and energetic imbalances that can be affected by spiritual intervention. In the capacity of healers, or medicine persons, shamans journey on behalf of their patient/client to the spirit world to meet with their helping spirits. While there, they use Spirit guidance and an array of techniques to diagnose illness etiology and restore wholeness and power to the person. The shaman usually expresses the wisdom offered from the spirit world to the client to help them on their path of healing and living in balance.

Animism and the Web of Life

Two central beliefs are found in all shamanic cultures: the belief in animism and belief in the interconnected web of energy and power between all things, called the Great Web of Life.

Animism is the understanding that all things—trees, mountains, wind, elements, animals, this book, the chair you are sitting in, and you and me—are living, are manifestations of the Web, are connected to the Web, and are souls. We are all created from, and filled with, life-force energy.

The Web of Life is the life-force energy that is the prime mover, or the essence of life. Life-force energy is a free-flowing, high-vibration energy that is the foundation of everything. It is omnipresent and is the essence of all things, a subtle undercurrent of all that is. Everything that is, is *alive* with life-force energy, and this same life-force energy is a connecting force between all things. The Web of Life radiates and pulses with this all-pervading energy. When we observe light, we see that it is made up of a broad spectrum of frequencies, some of which we can see, some of which are invisible to us.

Helping Spirits

The emanations and manifestations of the Web of Life are similar in that some are very dense, having a solid, physical form, while others are not. The Web is known to be alive, spirited, animated, and full of living beings that are visible and invisible to ordinary perception. Shamans are trained to see and sense the Web and its inhabitants using bare awareness, that place where our mind falls silent with inner knowing. In the ordinary world, manifestations of the Web are visible as beings and objects. Nonordinary world manifestations of the Web are generally not perceived as visible by most people. There are other worlds around us that in actuality aren't separate worlds, yet they remain invisible. These Otherworlds (discussed in detail in chapter three) are filled with manifestations of the Web that are made of more subtle, less dense energy, commonly referred to as spirits. Shamans work with these manifestations of the Web in powerful practice for healing, guidance, and enlightenment.

We all have guardian spirits, known in shamanism as helping spirits, spirit teachers, spirit allies, and/or power animals. Many people familiar with working with spirits refer to these as spirit guides or totems. For ease of reading, we will refer to these power sources with the all-encompassing term of helping spirits. Helping spirits are spirit energies that appear in diverse ways. They may appear in forms that are angelic, human, alien, energy being, animal, bird, reptile, insect, plant, or crystalline. Ancestors, past shamans and healers, gods and goddesses, ascended masters, prophets, sages, hierophants, alchemists, and teachers of varying cultures, paths, and mythologies often present themselves as helping spirits. Shamanic cultures believe everyone is born with at least one helping spirit that protects them and shares its power with them. Neo-shamanism pioneer Michael Harner has documented that connections to helping spirits increase one's physical energy and ability to resist disease, as well as increasing mental alertness and self-confidence.

Energy Bodies

The physical world is the densest energetic level on the Web of Life's energy spectrum; it is formed of subtler etheric energies that have coalesced and increased in density. To one degree or another, every physical person, place, or thing retains a characteristic energy signature, or a soul, from the higher realms. The energy body is what shamans call the radiance the soul creates in and around the physical body. In human beings, this energy body permeates and surrounds the physical one, and those who perceive it see it as a luminous egg that infuses and cocoons the body. The energy body appears to be bolted to the physical one via a series of energy vortices present along the spine. These vortices or bolts are traditionally known as chakras. They have been demonstrated by various Eastern arts, most notably Kundalini, to monitor and maintain different vibrational energy layers within the human energy body/field. Shamans know that the soul and luminous energy body are just as critical to health and well-being as a person's physical body. If a person's soul is not whole or the person's luminous energy body is dulled, weakened, or punctured by such things as draining or blocked energy, the person will experience power loss, imbalance, and disharmony that eventually causes illness and disease.

Awareness

Shamans know that to be capable of entering the spirit worlds and to effectively help others heal their souls and luminous energy bodies, they themselves must be as balanced, brilliant, clear, and whole as possible. Shamans working in service to the community must constantly look within themselves to clear away thoughts, emotions, behaviors, and energetic debris that can clog and diminish their luminous energy body. This clearing is done through vigilant bare awareness. This awareness, both internal and external, is perhaps the most important attribute to practicing shamanism. Shamanic teachers and helping spirits work in partnership with the shaman to help them with this process.

Shamans and people of shamanic cultures are acutely aware of themselves, each other, their surroundings, the spirits, and the Great Web of Life. Their survival has depended on this skill, and so will ours in the coming age. The world we live in is a manifestation of the Web and is in itself an intelligent being that communicates with us in every moment. Observing and listening to its subtle messages provides key information and insights into one's self and world.

Impeccability and Gratitude

While shamans use a variety of techniques and methods for healing and expanded awareness, an overwhelming guiding approach combined with an essential attitude carries them through the darkest of times and the most devastating lessons. Shamans honor their own spirit as they honor the spirits of all other beings with *impeccability* and *gratitude*.

There are many different ways to approach life and to interact with those around us. We've all seen the T-shirts or bumper stickers touting such worldviews as "Looking Out for Number One!" or "Think Globally, Act Locally." But no matter how lofty or base the approach is, it can be lived impeccably, if it is the expression of that person's soul in the world.

Impeccability has nothing to do with right and wrong. It does not involve the Buddhist tenets of Right Living or the Christian Golden Rule. What shamanic impeccability demands is the unflinching and focused expression of the soul's agenda. In the course of our training, we met the sweetest, most loving teacher in the world. We also met the least cordial, most demanding, overbearing tyrant you could ever want to meet. Both of these people acted impeccably. They expressed the soul according to their energetic nature in order to unerringly produce a substantive and enhancing increase in awareness in their students. They did so by addressing reality as it is and by being brutally honest with us as students. Neither of them was brutal by any means, but they exercised honesty like a laser beam, cutting away the illusion and the fatty self-indulgence from the minds of their charges.

Impeccability demands that we remain true to the expression of the soul. The soul appears to operate within certain guidelines: It does not purposely wound or hurt another's soul-self. Properly expressed, it is not cluttered or colored in any way by individual bias, opinion, or judgment. The soul, always awake, expresses the message, or series of messages, that will awaken the individual still held in thrall by the dream of illusion. The soul's message, and therefore the nature of impeccability, communicates the real.

The great sages who teach the importance of impeccability aren't telling us that we have to be the model citizens of our communities. They are teaching us to be internally consistent within ourselves. When we do something that is not true to our natural self, we lose energy, personal power, and vitality. This betrayal of self sits in direct opposition to the shamanic goal of living in balance, harmony, and economy with one's self and the Web. Impeccability is not perfection; it is consistently applied soulfulness that is born from a centered balance. To be impeccable, we need to know and honor our soul. This requires being awake and aware, genuine and real with ourselves and with others. This impeccability is accomplished by seeking to know and integrate our inner nature, connecting and staying connected with our self and helping spirits, and employing our soul guidance as we walk our life path. When we are impeccable with our self, it is easier for us to interact impeccably with others and the Web.

One of the reasons the shaman is compelled to express the soul in this way is gratitude. As painful and glorious as it can be, stripping away illusion and leaving ourselves awake and aware for the first time in our life, able to perceive the soul's purpose and express it in the world, leaves us profoundly grateful and eager to pass along that gift of awareness to others. Once the clutter of petty concerns is removed, we can see life's beauty, sacredness, and rarity. We are privileged to be wrapped in skin at this time, during this age of great transition and awakening. We have been gifted with the opportunity to explore our self, to delve deeper into the mysteries of life and the universe, and by doing so, to make a substantive difference in the world and our community.

Grace, impeccability, and gratitude are woven by intent into a beautiful braid that frames the face of a balanced and harmonious life. To live impeccably is to be whole and to honor our soul and the Web. When we are aware that all things exist and have great value, we experience gratitude. Gratitude is not an obligation, but rather an outpouring of feeling from the heart and soul. Life is sacred and honored by the shaman. To wake up thankful for another day of life on this beautiful planet is just one example of gratitude. We live in a throwaway, industrial, material society that has lost gratitude and respect for the world and its joys and blessings. Even life itself has been devalued through war, crime, and even the insurance-company concepts of "acceptable risk" and "collateral damage." Shamans never, ever forget the value of life, of soul, and of nature, and they express gratitude for these things with heartfelt prayer, offerings, and daily acknowledgment. To walk the shamanic path, we must open our hearts and give thanks often. You can start right now.

Exercise: Giving Thanks

Take a few moments to sit quietly and think about all of the blessings in your life. What are you thankful for? Your family, pets, safe home, friends, employment, vacation, health, mental acuity, leisure-time pleasures and pursuits, worldly comforts, good food and drink, music, art, sports, community, education, accomplishments, challenges, personal growth? What about the beauty of nature and the Earth? How about your life? How about your self?

Say a prayer of thanksgiving now in your own way. Give thanks to the Web of Life, or whatever source of life you choose, for making it all possible.

CHAPTER TWO

Paying Attention

*The world is full of obvious things which
nobody by any chance ever observes.*

—Sir Arthur Conan Doyle

One of the most dismissive statements in our language is one we hear with such frequency that we have become numb to it. It's a simple phrase and an occasionally necessary one, but it cuts us off from illumination. It is the statement, "I know." When someone says that, two things are certain. The first is that they want to conclude the event. The second is that they, indeed, do not know very much at all. "I know" is a phrase people use to end conversations, to establish hierarchy, to massage the ego. It is also used to exclude others from their perceived reality and to separate themselves from anyone else's.

We are at a point on the wheel of time where what we don't know can kill us. What we don't know is right around the corner, waiting to swallow us whole. We cannot indulge in the arrogance of what we think we know. What we think we know is largely irrelevant or demonstrably not working very well. What we don't know is a universe so vast as to boggle the mind. We do not have the time to indulge in our petty arrogances or in what we think we know. We need to move directly to the means of finding out what we need to know to make a difference with ourselves and the world and how to apply that knowledge.

At this point, take a moment and ask yourself why you are interested in shamanism. What is drawing you to this path? Look deeper. Is it an impulse or merely curiosity? Maybe research or a recommendation brought you to this door. Perhaps you just can't stay away.

One thing is certain. We can assure you that because you have picked up this book, no matter the circumstances or reasons, at some point in your life, you have been presented with the call of the Spirit. How do we know? Because it is a universal truth that those who are brought to a path of illumination — *any* path of illumination — have long been pursued by Spirit. They are just too self-absorbed or caught up in the world to see it for what it is. This is not an indictment — merely a fact. Everybody is a conduit of the Spirit, in every moment, all the time. They are part of the greater whole of life-force energy and therefore express that energy with their very being. But they don't know it. They are so caught up in the day-to-day or in their own internal story and personal history that they just don't have the time or the desire to pay close enough attention.

The call of the Spirit is generally some event in which the soul takes over and lets you know it is waiting for you to recognize it and move forward. It can be a miraculous event, such as when you live through something that should have killed you, or a much subtler, still, small inner voice whispering intuitive insight in your mind. Or it could merely be a magical experience that made you think there might be more to the universe than what you can see. In any case, Spirit crossed your path in a most obvious way. You have heard the call of the Spirit, and whether you know it or not, the result of that call has brought you here, to this book. In essence, you are in the middle of an event, and that event is the struggle of your soul to express itself in the world. You need to realize a few things in order for that to happen. The fact that you may not have realized that Spirit has been pursuing you for some time is where we need to begin.

The times we live in and the days to come require that we pay attention to what is going on. It might not seem like it, but paying attention is a radical and subversive act. It always has been, and it is even more so now. We are conditioned in our culture to *not* pay attention. We are told what to think, how we should act or dress, and what we should consider to be important. We are even told what to fear and what to love. We are told everything we need to know. And what we are told is designed to influence and manipulate us. Justifications for wars or civil-liberties violations, contrite apologies from politicians or religious leaders caught in disgrace, and national security-alert levels are all reported to us to achieve a tone, a feeling in society that directs our attention to a specific point, rather than where we might look if left to our own devices. Paying close attention allows us to observe what is really going on. It eliminates editorial slant, political spin, and media influence. In essence, it reveals the real and dismisses the illusion. Paying attention subverts those who would shape public opinion, those who would tell us what is to be believed to be true. Casting our observation inward to distinguish between what is truly real and what we merely think is real also subverts our own egos. Paying attention is a fundamental shamanic skill that must be cultivated. The path to being our own shaman and unleashing the power that we alone can wield begins with paying attention—to the world around us, to events, and to the nature of the self.

Shamanic training traditionally begins with observing nature. Wild nature is the pure expression of soul, of undiluted life-force energy, in the world. By deeply observing nature, we are presented with the efficiency, the grandeur, the humor, and the simplicity of life. We also begin to see that many of the things we hold in our thoughts are illusions, and many of our behaviors are ways that we, with great complexity, orchestrate the wasting of our own energy. What stands between our soul and the outside world is the reason we waste, the reason we self-sabotage.

•••

The azure blue sky speckled with cotton-ball clouds begged her to come out and play. Making her way gingerly to the pond, she remorsefully gazed up at the mountain. How she longed to hike the wooded trails to the meadow plateau and scenic vista! Confined to the edge of this water-lily world by her ailing body, she considered the nature of the illness—the whys, wherefores, and what-to-dos. She desperately wanted to become free of its ravages and admitted aloud to the bass swimming by that she would do anything—*anything!*—to be able to swim and hike and feel good again. She laughed at herself and wondered how she had gotten so desperate that she would talk to a fish about her problem.

And then it happened, right there on the dock in the silence between her cries of despair—the fish answered her back. Looking her square in the eyes and moving his mouth as fish often do, he responded.

"So you would do anything, you say? Anything? Are you sure? Would you be willing to take full responsibility for your illness, your imbalance, and your wounded soul? Would you be willing to take full responsibility for your life, your health, and your wholeness? Would you be willing to search for and find the healer within yourself? Would you be willing to follow your own advice? Are you ready to let yourself know that *you* are the cure that you are looking for? It's time! Stop looking outside of yourself and do your inner work."

The fish's mouth stopped moving, but his gaze was unbroken. In the stillness she pondered these ideas.

"Even if I am my own cure," she thought," I have no idea how to heal myself and be responsible for all of these things. It's too much; it's far too big." And then she stopped herself. "This is *me, my* life, *my* self. If I don't know, and if it's too big for me, and if I am not willing to do the work, then how can I expect someone else to do it for me? Yes, I need to heal myself. I have to heal myself. I can heal myself. I *will* heal myself."

What a realization! The feeling of it resonated through her body, and she felt more energy than she had felt in a long time. She didn't yet know how she was going to do it, but she knew the teachers and the ways would come now that she was primed for the learning.

"Thank you, Bass," she said with a nod. "And thank you, Me."

The Architecture of the Self

As mentioned earlier, we are hybrid beings, made up of body, mind, and soul. Of these three, body and mind are limited to this lifetime. With the soul being functionally eternal, it is easy to deduce that the soul is in a body for a reason, a purpose. The soul has an agenda and is using the body and mind as a way to interface with the world to attend to its agenda.

When we are born, we are pure soul sealed into an adorable little body. Over the next twenty-one years or so, we are steeped in everything we need to know to function in the world and in our society. Like little computers, we download programs from our family, school, church or religious group, peers, and seemingly endless media sources. These programs act as our software and applications, all overlaid on top of the still, small voice of our soul. All that programming stands between the soul we really are and the world. By the time we are adults, we are fairly well convinced that we *are* our programming. We are sure that the mask we are wearing to inter-face with the world is the totality of who we truly are.

Shamanism has long understood that the mind—or the thinking machinery, as it can be called—is loaded into us in a very orderly and sequential way, but modern brain and behavioral research has given us the language to understand it more completely. The behav-ioral software, or the sequential, orderly way the mind is loaded, is like a mask slowly built over our true nature. One model of the human thinking machinery includes four distinct developmental stages. These stages correspond directly to brainwave frequencies in very nearly a one-to-one correlation.

From birth to age three and a half, and as we develop brain fre-quencies from 0 to 3.5 cycles per second (cps)—or *delta*, as this span of brain frequencies is called—we begin to make the transition from a purely spirit-being to a physical spirit/human hybrid. We learn the rules of this plane of existence. We learn what is real, in other words. We learn what to believe in. These beliefs range from purely practical considerations, such as gravity and hot and cold, to more obscure things, like what we believe to be good or bad. We further download the beliefs surrounding who we are and what is expected of us. We learn how we should treat each other and how we deserve to be treated. These beliefs lay the foundation for the balance of our lives.

From ages three and a half to seven, and brainwave frequencies 3.5 to 7 cps, called *theta* frequencies, we learn all about our emo-tions. Emotions are those things that move us. They make us do things, compelling us to action. A typical theta reaction would be fight or flight. Love and courage, as well as virtually all of what we would consider deadly sins (avarice, avoidance, desire, anger, jealousy, over-indulgence, pride/entitlement) and an understanding of all these programs, are loaded into us during this period. We also write many of the emotional programs that are designed to defend the beliefs we established between birth to age three and a half. For instance, if at age two we come to believe that Daddy loves our sister better that us, then we will most certainly write a few behavioral programs to deal with that belief. Those programs/behaviors could include acting out or perhaps being especially cute and flirtatious; they will be idiosyncratic to the individual person and conform to the framework of other beliefs of what may be acceptable within the family unit. Theta is where we hold much of our pain and hurt from the circumstances of our youth, along with our joy and wonder.

From ages seven to fourteen, during development of frequencies 7 to14 cps, or *alpha* frequencies, we learn all about feelings. Feelings are different from emotions in that feelings are sensations of the mind, while emotions move us to action. Feelings are intuited observations. They are not logical nor do they move us to action. They are sensations only. This is the fundamental distinction between alpha and theta.

Emotions are enormous behavioral programs that dictate what we do. Feelings are smaller programs that dictate what we sense and feel in certain situations.

As an example, there may be many alpha sensations that we experience as we enter an old abandoned house: the feeling of creepiness, unease, uncertainty, dislike of the dark, unfamiliar territory; all may contribute to, but are not the same as, the fear that makes us run out of the house screaming. Alpha responses are all of the feelings we have, but the theta response is the one that makes us run, and coincidentally, validates the feelings we have. Because this distinction between alpha and theta is often difficult for people to immediately grasp, we offer another, more pleasant example. Alpha responses in dating might include enjoying the way your date looks or the way her hair smells. You may experience a thrill when you hear her laugh or listen to her voice on the other end of the phone. You may enjoy your conversations with her or find yourself missing her or longing for her presence when she is not around. These are all alpha responses to your sweetheart. But, none of these things necessarily move you to action.

Theta steps in when you get down on your knee and ask her to marry you. When you pledge to love, honor and cherish her in sickness and in health, and then DO it, you are acting from the theta response of love and honor. So, theta responses are those that make you do, whereas alpha responses are those which cause you only to feel.

During this phase, we feel "vibes," along with things like friendliness, warmth, fondness, and apprehension. The programs for what we like or don't like, what we think is creepy or enjoyable, and for what to do with all these mental sensations generally are written during this period. Keep in mind that the programs written in alpha are always in line with the controlling emotional theta programs, which reflect and defend the beliefs we hold to be true.

The final stage of development occurs from ages fourteen to twenty-one, during the building of the frequencies 14 to 21 cps, called *beta* frequencies. This period is designed to deal with logic. Practicality, priority, sequencing, reason—all these things finish loading and are cemented during this period. Beta is the topmost consciousness layer and the one we generally use to interface with the world. It is our day-to-day mind, the one that gets us up in the morning, moves us through our day, and gets us back home at night.

Shamanic teacher John Worthington, quoting brain researcher John C. Lilly, points out that, just like the programs in a computer, the programs that get loaded into us, along with the ones we write for ourselves based on our beliefs, emotions, and feelings, are the rules of our life until they are recognized and changed.[iii] After twenty-one years of loading in beliefs and programs into our thinking machinery, we get caught thinking that the programs are who we are. But who we are is really a soul having an organic human experience. Many people think we have or possess our souls, just as we might possess an SUV, a diamond ring, or the change in our pockets. They think they own it, not that they *are* it. This viewpoint is a typical product of operating from the programs rather than directly expressing the soul. The programs need not run our lives.

The key to uncovering the soul's agenda, its purpose in this life, and expressing that agenda in the world is to get underneath the programming and indoctrination heaped on us from birth and get back in touch with that pure soul. Once beneath this mask we've built, we need to clear a path from the soul, tunneling out into consciousness from delta to beta, so that the soul, not the mask, is the primary interface with the world. Don't think the ego or the mask was wasted time or energy, though. It serves a purpose. The mask gathers what we see and can translate into common parlance what emanates from the soul as it communicates with the world. The key is to allow the soul to use the ego/programs as tools, not to allow our entire being to be used as a tool of the ego/programs.

One way to begin this process is to unplug from the machine and get out into nature. Being in and contemplating nature provides a much needed shift in perspective. Nature wears no mask. It is primal and direct. There are no dichotomies in nature—no good/bad, right/wrong, happy/sad, foolish/wise. There is only the soul of nature, shining pure and clear. By placing ourselves in that environment, we can step aside from our programming and simply *be*. Faced with the masklessness of nature, our own mask falls away.

Cultivating Internal and External Awareness

To be effective shamans, we must become intimately aware of our worlds, both internal and external. We acquire this awareness by experiencing, not just reading. So we ask you now to take another experiential step. Take a few moments to think about the information that you have read so far. Notice what you think and feel about it. Take your time, and when you are ready, become aware of your intentions and motivations for embarking on this path by again asking yourself this question, "Why have I come to shamanism?"

Don't skip over this exercise. Bare awareness is the key to walking this path. Personal intention and self-awareness are paramount. Be open and honest. What are your motivations for becoming your own shaman? What are your goals? What are your priorities? Examine your thinking machinery. What are your feelings about this path (alpha)? What and how have you been moved to shamanism (theta)? What are your beliefs (delta)? By answering these questions honestly to the best of your ability for right now, you have begun one part of the shamanic quest: awakening to your internal world.

To become your own shaman you also need to develop an awareness of your external world, including the energies and spirits that move in all things. Energy, even strong energy, is subtle and therefore often unseen and unfelt by most people. This is part of the reason why it has taken science hundreds of years to confirm its existence. But the trained shaman using bare awareness can observe energy and spirit quite easily. Our goal is to develop and hone these abilities in ourselves so that we too can perceive and receive energy and spirit. This is what will make you your own shaman. Whether you are conscious of it or not, you already have the natural ability to do this.

You most likely have sensed your connection with energy and Spirit, though like the call of the Spirit, you may not have been aware of it. The following personal example may stimulate your awareness and memories of connection.

For many summers, Colleen has been blessed with being able to travel to picturesque northern Canada to explore the virgin forests and pristine waters of Lake Superior. The following journal entry describes an experience of being deeply engaged and sensing the Great Web of Life and life-force energy in nature.

The quiet, clean, fresh air is free from the noises of human life, and the boundless sky unencumbered by lights and smog. The long pebbly beach dotted with driftwood and colorful rocks provides much needed solitude from the stresses of my busy life. The occasional eerie loon calls, the wind through the majestic pines, and the rhythmic lapping of the great lake as she caresses the shore are the only sounds I hear. The power of the great lake permeates my awareness, even though to-day her layers of deep blue are calm. The gentle, rhythmic waves reach into my body and soul and move deep in my center. All of my senses validate the life-force energy within me. I feel peaceful, powerful, and connected to the beauty around and within me. Over the rugged sheer cliffs to my left I see minute bubbles forming tiny, winding, formless im-ages against the pinkish orange ribbons painted in the west-ern sky. The vision seems surreal, and I know that I have opened my senses into the realm of Spirit energy. Lost for many moments, the growling of my stomach reminds me that it is time to build the campfire to prepare my dinner back at camp. Later that night, snuggled in my sleeping bag, the rhythm and the images continue to move through me as I drift in deep slumber.

Now it's your turn. Most people find it easiest to develop their per-ception to be able to see, sense, experience, and feel energy and Spirit by becoming quiet inside themselves. Take a few moments right now to relax, draw in a few deep breaths, and connect. Af-ter reading this paragraph, close your eyes. Imagine yourself in one of your favorite places in nature, perhaps a park, garden, forest, ocean, or lake. Recall all of the feelings and sensations that you have had while in this place, and allow yourself to really feel them now. See, feel, sense and experience yourself there. Notice any sounds or smells. Take as much time as you can and fully experience all of the many sensations. When you are finished, take in a deep breath and open your eyes. Notice what you feel. What did you experience? How deeply were you able to connect with the energy and the spirit of this place? If you had difficulty with this exercise, that's okay; your skills will improve with practice.

Some people's natural ability to connect may have become lost or hidden through our culture's process of indoctrination used to produce educated, responsible citizens that generate some kind of work or product. We were told that daydreaming or seeing our invisible friend was wrong, so many people shut down their connection gifts. Because you already have the natural ability to connect, it isn't hard to retrain yourself to become receptive. You need only cultivate, activate, and enhance these natural skills. Practicing the journeys and exercises in each chapter of this book will help you learn how to connect and hone this ability into a practical skill for use in your everyday life.

Five-Step Process for Bare Awareness

Relaxation and the conscious silencing of mind chatter are typical avenues for opening to perception. When first beginning to awaken your energy-sensing abilities, you will experience the most success when you are relaxed and quiet physically, mentally, and emotionally. You can achieve this relaxation through the following five-step process, which cultivates a state of mindful bare awareness: (1) *setting your intention*, your desire to become calm and quiet, (2) *focusing*, mindfully directing your attention and placing your thoughts on relaxing, (3) *releasing*, stopping mind chatter and everyday, worldly thoughts, (4) *allowing*, permitting yourself to be fully present in the experience and to be receptive to all of the feelings, sensations, and insights that come to you during this time, and (5) *accepting*, performing all steps without judgment or analytical censoring.

In this state of mindful, bare awareness you can access one of the most potent faculties you have for perceiving energy and Spirit: your *felt sense.* Your felt sense is the combination of all of the feelings, sensations, and realizations that you experience at any given time from your multiple senses. To become conscious of your felt sense, notice what you feel everywhere in your physical body, paying particular attention to the center of your torso. Notice everything that you are thinking, then everything that you are feeling. Then notice what you feel energetically inside and around your physical body, then what you feel intuitively. Finally, notice everything in your whole being all at once. You don't have to be aware of every tiny nuance going on within you to experience your felt sense. (In fact, doing so would be quite impossible at this stage.) Rather, to become conscious of your felt sense, just be aware and notice the overall feelings, sensations, and realizations of all of the individual senses working collectively within you. Notice the undercurrent of energy flowing through this experience. This is your personal energy. You will use this skill throughout this book and your whole life, so be sure to take your time and really connect with your felt sense. Do this exercise often and notice the bare awareness that naturally shines through.

Used in addition to paying attention to your thoughts and motivations, this powerful felt sense will help you become aware of your internal world. You will also use it to perceive the energies and spirits in the external world. Let's begin practicing this perception by focusing on an object that is physically present in your environment. Interestingly, this same intense observational skill is the one psychic readers apply when reading a person's energy and potential energy.

Exercises: Developing Bare Awareness

These exercises will help you achieve bare awareness of your internal and external worlds using your everyday, ordinary state of consciousness. This bare awareness is crucial to becoming your own shaman. In fact, over time you will begin to notice that when people speak you are able to sense where in their thinking machinery — beta, alpha, theta, or delta — they are talking from. What programs they may be running and if they are telling the truth or not will become obvious to you when these senses are developed and you pay attention. By honing these skills, you will also be able to more effectively utilize and implement the energy and guidance that you will receive from Spirit while in shamanic journeying's altered state of consciousness.

Exercise One: Felt Sense

Choose an object that is near you, that you can see right now, to use as a focal point for sensing energy. Sit comfortably where you can see the object and gaze at the object with your eyes open. Use the five-step process and notice the messages you receive from your felt sense. Set your intention to relax. Release your mind chatter and allow your mind and emotions to become quiet. Take in a deep breath and relax your body.

Drop down out of your thinking mind and into your body by surrendering your thoughts and sending your attention into your body, heart, and soul. Some refer to this action as sinking into the second attention. A simple physical movement to help you accomplish this is to reach up and put your hands on your head. Gather the energy from in and around your head and sink it down into your body and energy field by moving your hands down the front of your body and bringing them to rest on your heart, then your solar plexus just under your rib cage, and then on your belly. Notice what you feel. Allow yourself to relax into your body.

Once you have become relaxed, mentally focus your intention on sensing the energy in the object you have chosen. Intentionally open up all of your senses and allow yourself to feel, visualize, and perceive the energy. It may help to soften your eyes. Feel with your felt sense—don't just think with your head. Notice what you are experiencing. Notice all of your sensations. Take your time.

When you can sense the object, receive this energy by allowing it to flow into you and through you. Take in a deep breath and open your body, mind, and personal energy field. Consciously draw in the energy without judgment or conditions, accepting everything that you notice and feel. Continue to draw in the energy for as long as you have time. When you are finished, don't shut back down. Try to stay open for as long as you can and remain aware of the different sensations you are having. Staying open will help you be more aware of energy and spirit in your everyday life.

To illustrate, Colleen offers a brief example of this exercise:

> I choose to connect with the energy and spirit of a freshly bloomed dandelion. I relax, use the five-step process and sink into my second attention. I notice that the golden yellow vibrates in my solar plexus and feels warm like the sun. I feel that the dandelion is happy to be blooming and soaking in the sun. A gentle breeze blows, and the dandelion dances on her milky stem. I recall the bitterness of childhood taste-testing and remember the yellow pollen being rubbed onto my chin and nose. I pay attention to all of these sensations of my felt sense and allow them to resonate in my awareness. I draw in the energy and spirit of the dandelion and feel that I too am happy to be blooming and soaking in the warm sun.

All of Colleen's felt-sense sensations took about thirty seconds. Practicing longer would have provided the opportunity to learn more about the dandelion and experience deeper sensations.

This very same technique can be used to access energy and spirit anywhere. Colleen's description of her trip to Lake Superior is another good example of this exercise in action. At first you can most easily perform this exercise in a quiet place where you will not be interrupted, particularly in natural locations. However, energy and spirit are everywhere and can be accessed anywhere.

Another way to begin practicing your felt-sense skill is to choose a place that works for you. An outdoor location that is quiet and where you can be alone and undisturbed is ideal. For example, you might go to a local nature preserve and lie on a blanket, or you could simply sit in a lawn chair in your back yard. Once you are there and have made yourself comfortable, take in several long, deep breaths and allow yourself to go even deeper into relaxation. Use the five-step process of setting your intention, focusing, releasing, allowing, and accepting, and open up all of your senses as you continue to relax. Sink into your second attention.

With open eyes, "look" around with your felt sense. Explore. Notice what you see. Notice what you think. Notice what you sense. Notice what you feel. Notice everything together. There are no right or wrong sensations. Every person's experience is unique, and whatever happens is right for you. Be aware of all of your senses. Sometimes people feel energy and spirit as a rushing sensation, a tingling or pulsating, or a temperature fluctuation, such as a chill or a glow of warmth. For others the feeling is calm and smooth. Some people smell different scents associated with the energy of the spirits, such as incense, sage, Grandpa's pipe smoke, or the musky scent of their power animal's fur. Some people hear sounds like voices, music, singing, and chanting. Some people see spirit energy images in their mind's eye. Some people feel emotional sensations. Some people experience physical sensations. This response does not happen in your head from thought; it occurs in the felt sense of your body and energy field. Be open to whatever you experience. Take your time and really embrace the experience. The deeper you are able to go, the more energy you will be able to harvest for yourself.

Exercise Two: Still Point

It is difficult to connect with energy and spirit when we are stressed, agitated, preoccupied, or full of mind chatter. Yet these are some of the times that we could most benefit from an energy and spirit connection. To help calm yourself and open the connection channels, we recommend this exercise to connect with your inner still point.

Deep within us, as deep in the thinking machinery as delta, is a reservoir of peace called the *still point*. It is like a calm, peaceful, placid lake, serene and tranquil, a place so devoid of tension and stress that thoughts do not exist there. We can reach this place by intentionally quieting our thoughts and feelings. Once we are adept at visiting this place within, we can achieve a state of consciousness that long-term meditators train themselves to enter and hold for hours. Even if you don't have hours to spend in this place, you can access multitudes of benefits through short visits.

Begin this exercise by making yourself comfortable and closing your eyes. Sit or lie down—it's up to you. Use the five-step process of setting your intention, focusing, releasing, allowing, and accepting, and as you relax, open up all of your senses to experience and feel the energy and spirit connection. Inhale slowly and deeply, and as you exhale, allow all of your worries, stresses, and thoughts to exit with your breath. Inhale again, even more slowly and deeply than before, and as you exhale, allow the stress and tension in your muscles to exit your body. Feel yourself becoming more relaxed. Inhale deeply and slowly once more, allowing all of your emotions to exit with your exhalation. Drop into your second attention by relaxing your thinking mind. If you need to, pull the energy out of your head and draw it down into your center with your intention. Focus your awareness on the energy flowing through and around your head. Gather that energy into a ball and sink it down into your center.

Become quiet—no thoughts, no feelings, just quiet. Feel the quietness with your felt sense. Allow yourself to become completely and totally still. Just be.

As you sit quietly, bring your awareness to your core, your deep center. Allow yourself to experience the relaxation and inner calm of no thought. Go as deeply into your center as you can, and be aware of your inner stillness. Connect with that still point within. Don't do anything, don't think anything. Fall between the cracks of your thoughts and feelings and allow yourself to simply exist. Lose your-self. Totally let go of everything—your thoughts, your emotions, any physical sensations, and your sense of being in a physical body. Just be still. You are nothing but your life-force energy.

Experience this quietness for as long as you have time for, and then return to ordinary reality by gently opening your eyes and tak-ing in a deep breath. Notice how you feel. Ask for an image, a pic-ture, or a metaphor to come to mind that represents your still point. In the future you can use this image to help transport you to your still point more quickly or help you go more deeply into it.

In addition to helping you relax into a receptive state of con-sciousness, this exercise is also an effective stress-reduction tool. By taking just a few minutes periodically throughout the day to connect with your inner still point, you can instantly release the tension in your body, thoughts, and emotions and replenish yourself with the quiet stillness that brings balance and harmony back into your life.

Exercise Three: Truth Spot

Another important awareness skill significant in shamanism is feel-ing truth in your body and felt sense. This skill provides an excel-lent barometer to your thoughts and feelings. Once you hone it, you will be able to discern your truth through resonating affirmation, even when your ego demands to be in control or your emotions are clouding your judgment. The *truth-spot sensation* is used in many dis-ciplines and cultures; when people use phrases like "sit with," "let simmer," "let cook," "go within," and "gut feelings," they are often accessing the truth-spot sensation. When you quiet the busy mind, focus on a situation or issue, and become aware of how this situa-tion or issue makes you feel, you are accessing your inner guidance, through physical sensation, to discern your truth and healthiest course of action.

Begin this exercise by sitting quietly and clearing your mind and center. Close your eyes. Use the five-step process of setting your intention, focusing, releasing, allowing, and accepting. Inhale slowly and deeply, and as you exhale, allow all of your worries, stresses, and thoughts to exit with your breath. Inhale again, even more slowly and deeply than before, and as you exhale, allow all of the stress and tension in your muscles to exit your body. Feel yourself become relaxed. Inhale deeply and slowly once more, allowing all of your emotions to exit with your exhalation. Now just become quiet, allow yourself to be still, and just be.

As you sit quietly, bring your awareness to your center. Allow yourself to experience relaxation and inner calm. Now make a statement to yourself you know to be true. Note the feeling that you have in your body when you do this. Note the exact spot(s) within you that resonates with the truth of this statement, and make a mental note of the tone of that feeling. Now make an untrue statement. Note the exact spot(s) within you that resonates with the truth of this statement, and make a mental note of the tone that spot may have. . . . Make a mental note of the place(s) in your body where this untruth spot exists, along with the spot's characteristic tone.

For example, if Colleen were doing this exercise, she would say, "My name is Colleen Deatsman." She would sit quietly and feel where in her body this statement of truth rings true and how that statement feels to her. Then she would make an untrue statement, such as, "My name is John Denver." She would then feel the difference in both the place and the tone of the resulting resonance within her, as well as being aware of how other areas in her body and felt sense are reacting. Many people report feeling warmth or a tingling sensation throughout their body that seems to be more concentrated in their solar plexus or heart when they speak the truth. When they speak an untruth, they report feeling constriction in the heart or in the pit of their stomach. Others feel a full-body, natural energetic repulsion to the statement that signals a felt sense red flag. Because each person is unique, individual responses will vary. We encourage you to practice and cultivate your awareness of truth and nontruth until you are comfortable trusting your internal discernment skills. Note the differences in your accuracy and inaccuracy at different times and when you are addressing different shadings of the truth. Often, your track record with this exercise will point to issues that you can then identify and understand within yourself. Very quickly, you will find that you are able to access this ability in the course of your everyday, busy life, even when quiet centering is not possible. Truth will always hit your truth spot, just as untruths will always hit your untruth spot. In this same way, you can also unerringly determine right from wrong and healthy from unhealthy.

If it was difficult for you to sense energy during these three exercises, that's okay. Don't get discouraged. Keep trying. What may now seem abstract and difficult to perceive can be seen, sensed, and felt in tangible ways with conscious intent and consistent practice. Keep in mind that when first developing your perception and reception skills, you will experience the most success in places where you can relax and where life-force energy is abundant. Soon you will be able to perceive and receive the energy of the Web of Life no matter where you are using your intention and awareness.

The journeying technique that you will learn in the next chapter is a technology of the sacred, which will help to open up the ordinary world and unveil the nonordinary world, thus allowing you to touch and perceive the Web of Life. Shamans use this technique to see, sense, and feel the interconnectedness of life and utilize this power and knowledge for the healing and guiding of others. In this same way, you, as a personal practitioner, can access the Web of Life to receive spiritual power to heal yourself, find guidance and wisdom, and activate personal energy.

The adventure awaits. Let's learn how to journey!

CHAPTER THREE

Journeying the Central Axis and the Three Otherworlds

*Shamanism is far too important to be left
in the hands of only the shamans.*

—Victor Sanchez, author and Toltec shamanism teacher[iv]

She lies in her soft space, resting and allowing the drumbeat to shift her awareness. Repeating the intention of her journey three times, she projects her presence to her departure point. The campfire in the wooded grove dances gaily into the sky and draws her into the dance. The power rises, and the energy rushes through her as her rhythmic two-step intensifies into a flowing whirl of ecstasy. The lift of the swirling energy gives way to feathers and wings that send her circling above the campfire as an eagle. Within moments she soars low over wildflowers and butterflies in a neighboring meadow and dives headfirst into a pool of shimmering water.

The refreshing water yields a tunnel of spiraling energy that carries her down into the Lower World. Dark and cool, the welcoming tunnel vibrates with the undulations of the heartbeat of Mother Earth. She passes quickly into the Lower World and is deposited in a landscape that reminds her of a place she once camped in the Wyoming Tetons. Towering, snowcapped peaks, virgin forests, pristine rivers, and deep, clear blue lakes greet her senses. Her power animal, the regal Bull Elk, meets her, and she immediately throws her arms around his neck in welcoming embrace.

Today the intention of her journey is to explore this Lower World healing place and to power-fill with earth and spirit energy. Hiking over mountain passes, forging great rivers, and frolicking in cold, crystal-clear lakes, her soul is filled with the satisfying food of nature, Spirit, and the Earth. The ecstasy she feels is profound, and her heart swells with gratitude. Energy courses through her veins, and she is vibrant and whole once more; the ravages of stress are gone from her world for now. Lazing in the pine-forested mountainside, she leans against the soft hair of her elk ally, feeling the strong power and protection he brings to her soul. He telepathically acknowledges her appreciation of their partnership, nodding her way. She is filled with the knowledge that she is healed by this love relationship with Spirit. The call-back drumbeat sounds, and she reluctantly bids farewell, expressing her deep gratitude and hurrying up the tunnel to the lake, the meadow, and the campfire. She gathers in all the energy of the journey and then returns to her body, lying peacefully in the soft space.

We live in a time of separation and disconnect from soul, Spirit, and life-force energy. Given the signs and portents, this disconnect is going to get worse before it gets better. But it doesn't have to be that way for everyone. Those who have the desire and determination can make a powerful change in their lives and world right now through the practice of journeying. Why live in misery or wait for things to get worse when we have a tool that makes a difference at our fingertips?

What the world needs most right now is wisdom, and journeying is the world's most ancient and effective wisdom tool. Journeying is not an escape or a trite practice. It is the act of gathering energy and power to make changes to real problems, issues, and imbalances that cause such things as illness, disease, pollution, stagnation, dissention, war, and intolerance. By harnessing and applying the power and wisdom of the Otherworlds, we have a direct line to the heart of our issues; we can discover and resolve them at the root cause. Now that's real power!

The Central Axis and the Three Otherworlds

The ancient and sacred technique of journeying entails entering an altered state of consciousness and allowing the soul to travel along a central axis to alternate realities, often referred to as Otherworlds, inner dimensions, spirit worlds, or spirit realms. These realms exist within and around us, just outside of our daily perceptions. They can be accessed through doorways, gateways, vortexes, and tunnels, all of which are known as *portals*.

When journeyers pass through a portal, they enter the *central axis*. The central axis isn't a place, but sacred space that is the center of the worlds and links the worlds together. It passes through every dimension and has openings into each of the Otherworlds. The central axis acts like a vacuum or an elevator, transporting journeyers to the Otherworld entrances. Parallels in nature are sweeping energy conduits such as the jet stream or the transatlantic current. Representations of the central axis appear across cultures and have varying depictions. It is commonly symbolized as a center pole or sacred pillar that can be ascended and descended, and is known by such names as the World Tree, Tree of Life, Golden Pillar, Middle Pillar, World Pillar, and Celestial Column. The Cosmic Mountain is another common representation of the central axis, and castles, churches, temples, and pyramids are built in its likeness.

Most shamanic cultures view the universe as having three levels: Earth, Underworld, and Sky. In core shamanism, as presented by Michael Harner and the Foundation for Shamanic Studies, the universe is divided into three worlds: the *Middle World*, *Lower World*, *and Upper World*. (We will refer to these three realms collectively as the Otherworlds.) All three of these worlds have multiple layers or levels within them. The Middle World, or Earth, is the world in which we live. It has both physical and spiritual aspects. The Upper World, or Sky, and Lower World, or Underworld, are places of spiritual power and high-vibrational energies where helping spirits reside. These worlds have nothing to do with religious delineations such as heaven or hell. It is beneficial to access these worlds for healing energy, divine guidance, and personal empowerment.

Where journeyers choose to go on their journeys depends upon their intention. As each journeyer is unique, the terrain of the worlds in which he or she travels is also unique. The exceptions are shamans trained to travel to culturally specific places in the Otherworlds. The worlds hold infinite possibilities of landscape, energies, helping spirits, and experiences. What you will experience in these worlds will vary based on your individual experiences, culture, training, needs, soul, and helping spirits, though journeyers are typically drawn to the places where their helping spirits live and work.

In the next three paragraphs, we briefly describe some common aspects of the three worlds from our journey and teaching experiences to give you an idea of what you might experience. Please remember that there are no ironclad descriptions or rules that define the energies, aspects, and characteristics of the Otherworlds. So it is important to release any expectations that you might have and trust that whatever your experience is, it is just right for you. If things appear contrary to your expectation, ask your helping spirits why. You might receive a valuable teaching about releasing expectations and things not always being what they seem.

The Lower World typically feels earthy and primal, so you may find that it looks and feels very much like Earth or places that you

know on Earth. It is generally elemental—that is, guidance, healings, energy, and power often come from the archetypal elements
like earth, air, fire, and water. It is common to meet many of your
power animals in the Lower World, though helping spirits of all
kinds can be found here. Many shamanic traditions believe that the
Lower World is the womb of Mother Earth. Common intentions
for journeying to the Lower world are grounding, centering, energy
cleansing, power filling, and healing.

The Upper World is generally observed as being ethereal with
a light, airy feel and high-vibrational energy that sometimes makes
one feel lightheaded upon returning from a journey to it. Many people experience velvety blackness and pastel or vibrant colors, like
blue, indigo, and purple, in the Upper World. Mountains, rainbows,
clouds, crystal temples, pulsating energy patterns, symbols, and cosmic matter are often observed. People report meeting helping spirits in human form and connecting with deceased ancestors, loved
ones, and pets. Some power animals can be met in the Upper World,
and mythical beings such as unicorns and winged horses also appear there. Meeting with angels and religious deities is also typical.
Common intentions for journeying to the Upper World are energy
cleansing, power filling, healing, guidance, wisdom, and teachings.

The Middle World is the world of our everyday life, having both
physical and spiritual aspects. It is unique in that the ordinary and
nonordinary worlds overlap in it. It is the world of balance and integration of perceptual dual opposites, like joy and suffering, pain
and passion, light and dark, good and bad, science and spirituality,
male and female, empowering and power-draining influences, and
so on. The Middle World is the place where energy vibrates at its
slowest rate. Here energy can stagnate, causing illness and despair,
or it can flow freely, creating health and joy, depending on the person's level of awareness and their energy-movement skills. Common
intentions for journeying in the Middle World are healing, self-soul

retrieval, energy retrieval, locating lost objects, connecting with nature or loved ones, energy clearing, energizing, and walkabouts (out-of-body work).

The Shamanic Trance State

A shaman or journeyer enters a trance state to access the Otherworlds. This ecstatic state is commonly termed the dreamtime, shamanic state of consciousness, and/or nonordinary reality. This state of deep awareness allows the journeyer to place the conscious, critical, left-brained mind at rest while exploring the realms of vast possibility in the Otherworlds. The trance state used by shamans and journeyers is the theta state of brainwave activity—the state that is the closest to sleep and the deepest conscious state most people can sustain closest to the soul interface in delta. Thus many shamans are called dreamers or are said to be dreaming the journey. This state feels similar to daydreaming, though it is much, much deeper. Journeyers often enter the shamanic trance with the assistance of monotonous rhythmic drumming, rattling, singing, chanting, non-lyrical music, movement, or verbal narration. Once the journeyer enters this state of consciousness, the journey begins.

The technique of journeying is natural, like dreaming, and everyone can journey if they want to. However, it utilizes certain skills that are not common in our busy society and may require honing before successful journeying is attained. Relaxation, imagination, focus of intention, concentration, and surrender are some of the skills needed. Relaxation and a quiet mind allow us to move from the ordinary world into the nonordinary world. Imagination is the vehicle that begins the journey and opens the portals that connect us with the nonordinary world. Focus of intention is the link that moves the imagination forward and into connection with the Web of Life. Concentration trips the conscious, critical mind, which judges, analyzes, and tries to sabotage our movement into nonordinary reality. Surrender allows us to go into the feeling of the moment without attachment to outcomes. It is not a giving up of your self, but a giving over to your soul and to the experience. It is loosening the tight grip we hold on our minds, bodies, and our perceptions of the world, and a relaxing of the need to be in control.

Successful journeying is so simple that it eludes us sometimes when we first begin. But through continued attempts and by honing the necessary skills, we usually meet with success. Sometimes we try so hard to will something to happen that it isn't able to flow. As you practice journeying, let go of your will to accomplish, relax, and just allow the energy to flow through you. Feel the expansion of your mind with this flow. Let go. Have fun. You may have a serious intent for your journey, but exploring the nonordinary world is a pleasant and joyful adventure. Relax and enjoy entering the world of personal healing and wisdom.

As just mentioned, imagination is the doorway we use to enter the journey. Our shamanic colleague Emery Forest once said, "To imagine is to visit the nation of images." These images are the dictionary we use to communicate with our soul selves when we dream. They are also the means by which we can communicate with helping spirits during a journey. We all have the ability to communicate with our soul selves and helping spirits using images. Each of us has an idiosyncratic language of images we employ in the process, a dream language based on our personal experiences. The mind makes connections between external stimuli and our emotional or situational response. Because these connections communicate a vast spectrum of information, the situation, the components of the situation, or the main players in the situation are images used by the soul and helping spirits to communicate with us.

Once we pass through the doorway of imagination, we utilize this language to maneuver and interact within nonordinary reality. Imagination starts the journey but is not the journey. It is the tool we use as we first move into ourselves, then into the Otherworlds.

Done properly, the imagination is the conveyance that ushers us into the realm of true experience. We are not fabricating what happens on a journey even though the images seem personal and familiar. How can they not, when we are employing our own personal dream language?

The Journey Process

Preparation

Before each journey it is helpful to ease yourself out of your everyday conscious mind by entering a soft space where you can relax and be comfortable. A soft space is any place where you feel calm, content, and at ease. This setting varies depending on personal needs and tastes. Some people like airy, sunny rooms with babbling fountains. Others prefer a cozy, dimly lit corner with soft drumming in the background, or an outdoor location in the woods, in a garden, or near a lake or river. The place that you choose is a special place because it is where your energy resonates. Create an environment that is warm, comfortable, and conducive to energy flow. Use soft blankets and plush pillows, if you like. If there is no such place in your home, perhaps there is a place in your vicinity—a meditation center, a reading room in the library, or a private room in your church. The place is of no consequence; how you feel there is.

Don't forget a tape or CD player with headphones or a drum or rattle, if you need them. Tapes or CDs of various sounds, such as repetitive drumming or rattling, can be purchased online, through mail order, and in many stores. Many journeyers prefer the sound and vibrations of live drumming or rattling and will drum or rattle for themselves on the journey or ask for an assistant to drum or rattle for them. Drumbeats and rattling at a certain meter will tend to drive your brain waves to theta frequency, allowing easier communication with your soul self and helping spirits.

Once you have entered your soft space, light a candle, but not too close to you, in case your body moves during the journey. Spirits of light are attracted to the flame. You might choose to use significant objects to create an altar around the candle. These items, known as *power tools*, can be natural items that you have found, special gifts, representations of helping spirits, or any items that represent Spirit in your life. (Acorns, pinecones, stones, feathers, and other items from nature honor Mother Earth and the nature spirits. Be sure not to injure trees, plants, or animals in your quest for power tools.)

Beginning the Journey

Once you have settled into your soft space, take a few minutes of quiet, alone time before beginning the journey. Make yourself comfortable, take in a deep breath, and relax. Drum or play some gentle drumming or instrumental music to help you unwind. Empty your mind of everyday thoughts, emotions, and distractions. In this more relaxed state of consciousness you will be more receptive to experiencing, feeling, visualizing, and sensing your journey. You will note that this act of intentional relaxation takes you out of your everyday mind in beta and helps you sink into the realm of feeling in alpha. Research has shown that placing your hands together in prayer position in front of your chest and looking up also drives your brainwaves deeper into an alpha rhythm.

When you feel ready, begin to shift your consciousness and call to the helping spirits using a rattle or drum. You may also choose to dance, sing, or whistle—whatever works for you. This brief ritual helps you to become present in the moment and open to connecting with Spirit. Some journeyers use this time to invoke their helping spirits and the energies and medicines in each of the directions of their personal medicine wheel. (There is more about helping spirits in chapter five and about personal medicine wheels in chapter six.)

Once you have begun to relax and open yourself to the spirits and the Otherworlds, state the intention of your journey. Your intention is very important because it establishes a purpose for the journey and makes it easier to interpret the messages received during the journey. Your intention can be anything. For example, a typical journey would be for healing or for guidance and wisdom regarding a particular subject or personal issue.

Turn on the CD or tape, lie down, and position yourself comfortably. You might choose to cover up with a blanket. You can also journey sitting or standing, if you prefer. Breathe deeply and calm yourself. Quiet your mind and let go of any concerns, thoughts, expectations, or fears. Cover your eyes with a bandana, an eye cover, or your arm for complete darkness. Breathe deeply and allow your mind and body to become calm.

Think of a place where you feel connected, safe, and protected—a special place where you enjoy spending time or did as a child. This can be an actual physical place or a place that you visit in your mind or daydreams that is not an actual physical location. This place is called your *departure point*. Visualize your departure point. Place yourself there as vividly as possible, using all of your senses to really experience yourself being there.

When you feel yourself there, think again of the intention for your journey and repeat your intention three times. This is very important as it focuses the energy of the journey.

During the Journey

Be open to using all of your senses and fully experience your journey. Suspend your conscious critical mind while allowing the witness part of your mind to remain open and aware of occurrences and details. Allow any thoughts or distractions that come into your mind to drift through. Though journeying is a serious spiritual practice, it is also fun, so enjoy the ride.

No matter what you "see" or experience, just relax, be aware, and allow the journey to unfold. Explore the terrain, if you see any, and "talk" with any helping spirits that you meet. Communication often occurs telepathically or comes into your mind as a "knowing." Because of the remarkable nature of spirit connection, all you have to do is think of questions to ask or things to say, and usually the answers come into your mind before you have finished formulating the questions. As mentioned earlier, you can interpret the images you see and the things you experience using your personal dream language. The more you journey, the more familiar you will become with the images the spirits use as they interact with you. Everything is relevant, so learn to pay close attention to all that you experience while on your journey.

In ordinary reality, we tend to rely heavily on vision to feed us most of the information we receive about our world, often to the minimization of our other senses. Our other senses continue to send us information, but we are often less aware of their input. In nonordinary reality, senses, such as feeling, sensing and knowing, which we may not normally recognize or interpret in ordinary reality, are opened and exercised. Because our mode of gaining information in nonordinary reality may not be visual, people may feel they did not achieve their journey destination or that they were unsuccessful in journeying. If you don't see anything, it does not mean that you are not journeying or that nothing is happening. Notice if you are hearing or smelling anything. Focus on your feelings and become aware of them. What sensations are happening in your body? Relax and allow all of your senses and your felt sense to come alive and bring their awareness to you. All that happens during a journey is important information for you to utilize in your healing, daily life, and spiritual evolution. Becoming multisensual is one of the powerful benefits of journeying and one that opens us up to intuition and spiritual guidance in our daily ordinary reality.

Returning from and Recording Your Journey

If you are listening to a drumming or rattling CD or tape, you will hear a repetitive beat that will change into a rhythm of seven beats

repeated four times. This callback beat alerts you that it is time to return to ordinary consciousness. When you hear the rhythm change,
thank any helping spirits that you have met and descend to your
departure point. Feel yourself back in your soft space and back in
your physical body. Stretch and wiggle to bring your essence all the
way back into your body. Be gentle with yourself as you return.

After your journey, again thank the helping spirits who had joined
you and let them know you are finished. Ponder the journey you just
experienced. Every detail in a journey has significance. Take a few
moments to write down your journey in a journal, documenting all
the details as best as you can recall.

Writing down the details is a very important step for personal
and spiritual growth, and it may help you find clarity with issues you
might not recognize otherwise. Buy or make a journal that appeals
to you. This journal becomes your companion, a "friend" that you
share all of your journey experiences with. Writing helps to focus
thoughts and allows the flow of information to come from you onto
the paper, so that you can see in words what is happening. Writing
also helps reveal the patterns and underlying beliefs important to
uncovering your soul.

As time and your journeys progress, it is important to look back
over the lessons and wisdom gained in past journeys. Sometimes we
are unable to gain clear understanding or process certain information at the time of the journey. As we progress in journey skills and
perhaps spiritual insight, we may be better able to understand what
guidance and teachings were being offered.

After documenting your journey, spend a few moments sitting
quietly in your soft space reflecting, reviewing, and interpreting. Jot
down these thoughts as well. Extinguish the candle, thanking the
Spirit of the Fire. Notice how you feel.

Journeying to the Otherworlds

For your first several journeys it is recommended that your intention be to travel to one of the Otherworlds, explore the terrain, feel that world's energy, and connect with your helping spirits in that world.

The Upper World

We specifically suggest visiting the Upper World on your first journey. An intention statement for that journey might be, "The intention of my journey is to travel to the Upper World; to meet with my helping spirits there; to sense, feel, and experience the energies there; and to explore the terrain of the Upper World." Repeat this sentence to yourself out loud or silently to yourself three times as you begin your journey. Take in another deep breath and relax.

Visualize yourself clearly at your departure point and find a way to go up. You will be traveling as spirit, so the rules of the physical do not apply; you can breathe underwater, float in the air, and squeeze into a tiny space. Some people climb a mountain, tree, or a vine similar to the one the childhood fable "Jack and the Beanstalk" (a classic Upper World shamanic account of European origin). Or you may fly to the Upper World as a winged being, such as a bird or insect, or be carried there by a flying being or with a storm similar to that depicted in *The Wizard of Oz*. Some people drift up like the smoke from a campfire, climb a rainbow, cross a rainbow bridge, float up in a hot-air balloon, or have an airplane speed them up. Some are sucked up into the realms of the Upper World with a vacuumlike action. Regardless of how you go, you are traveling along the central axis.

At the entrance to the Upper World you will pass through a porous boundary that separates the Middle and Upper Worlds. The appearance of the boundary varies. Typical descriptions include a thin sheet of plastic wrap or a stratum of water, colors, mist, or clouds. The boundary is not an obstruction, and most pass through it effortlessly, though some envision creating an entry point using a metaphysical tool, such as a crystal or pocketknife. Helping spirits assist others on their entry.

The Upper World landscape will appear different to all who journey, so relax and explore. Allow your journey to unfold, allowing yourself to surrender into the experience and enjoy it. Use all of your senses to fully experience everything. When the callback sounds to let you know it's time to return to ordinary reality, thank any helping spirits you have met and let them know you are finished. Look for a way to return to your departure point. It may be the same way you went up or it may be different. Either way, the portal will open up naturally for you so you can descend down through the portal, back to your departure point. Complete your journey as described earlier in the chapter, feeling yourself back in your body, reflecting on your experiences, and recording them in your journal.

The Lower World

You journey to the Lower World the same way you travel to the Upper, except that you travel down into the Earth, a la Alice in Wonderland (a Lower World journey account). Prepare yourself in the same way as described for the Upper World journey by creating a quiet sacred space, calling to the spirits, and settling into a comfortable journey position. Visualize your departure point strongly in your mind. Place yourself there as vividly as possible using all of your senses to really experience yourself there. Breathe deeply and relax. When you feel yourself there, think of the intention for your journey and repeat your intention three times. For your first several journeys it is recommended that your intention be to travel to the Lower World, explore the terrain, feel the energies, and connect with your helping spirits there. Take in another deep breath and relax.

Visualize yourself clearly at your departure point and look around for an opening into the Earth—anything that acts as a portal into the Earth and that feels right for you. This portal may be a rabbit hole, bee hole, snake hole, hole at the base of a tree—any kind of hole. Or you may prefer to descend through water by diving into a lake, river, waterfall, or whirlpool. Some people prefer going into the center of a flower or a tree and slipping down through the roots into the Earth, or going through the coals or the ashes of a campfire or the space between a rock and the Earth. Others are simply drawn down as if caught up in a waterslide or a mudslide. Remember, you will be traveling as spirit, so the rules of the physical do not apply. You can breathe underground, walk on water, and slide down a tiny hole.

Once headed down into the Earth, your portal turns into a tunnel. If at first the tunnel seems dark or dim, don't be afraid. It might go along the ground or under the ground. The tunnel may curve around, or it may descend steeply. Often the tunnel appears ribbed. Some people pass through the tunnel so quickly it is not seen. If the tunnel is too small or dark, widen it and brighten it. At this point in the journey, your imagination is still in control of your surroundings, and you can make your route into the Otherworld as comfortable for yourself as possible. At the end of the tunnel, you emerge into the Lower World. Relax and allow your journey to unfold. Surrender into the experience and enjoy your journey. Use all of your senses to fully experience everything.

The callback will let you know it's time to return to ordinary reality. At that time, thank any helping spirits that you have met and let them know you are finished. Look for the tunnel that will take you back to your departure point. It will reappear no matter how far you have roamed from its opening, or you will be instantaneously transported back to the opening. Ascend up through the tunnel, the portal in the Earth, and back to your departure point. Complete your journey as described earlier in the chapter, feeling yourself back in your body, reflecting on your experiences, and recording them in your journal.

The Middle World

The procedure for Middle World journeying is similar to that for Lower and Upper Worlds journeying, except that you will be traveling here, in the world in which you live, but in your spiritual form. It's like taking a mental or spiritual walk. You can journey from your departure point or from your soft space. You may meet helping spirits that you have already met on previous journeys, or you may meet new ones. It is important when journeying in the Middle World to ask questions of the beings you meet to be sure their intentions are for your highest good. In the Middle World, there are mischievous spirits, so use your wits and your senses and interview your new acquaintances. Do not allow this caution to frighten you from Middle World journeying, however; this is a very powerful healing technique, and there are many helping spirits and energies in the Middle World. Utilizing your senses simply assures that your journey will have the most advantageous outcome.

Prepare yourself and your soft space as you would for any journey. Visualize yourself in your departure point or fully present in your body and soft space. State your intention three times: "The intention of my journey is to meet with my helping spirits and journey in the Middle World to (such-and-such place), to do (such-and-such thing)." Relax and allow the journey to flow and unfold. Surrender into the experience and enjoy yourself. Use all of your senses to fully experience everything.

When it is time to return, thank any helping spirits that you have met, travel back over the landscape you previously traveled, and return to your body and your soft space. Become aware of your body, close your journey, and record your experiences and interpretations as you would for any journey.

Shamanic Ecstasy

When you return from a journey, you may feel joyful and light. *Shamanic ecstasy* is the term used to describe the high-vibration energy boost and euphoric high that many journeyers experience when they come out of a trance. This high is exquisite and defies description with mere words. Journeys are magical travels into the mysterious, where the journeyer connects with energy that is often electric and vibrates at a high frequency. This energy is an order above any energy here in our everyday world. The feelings elicited by this contact are intense, esoteric sensations that can be tangibly felt throughout the entire body. Upon returning from a journey, the traveler is both calm and supercharged at the same time. This energy connection heals our power-zapped, ravaged bodies and turns us into healthy, power-filled beings able to live vibrantly in our ordinary worlds and amidst the chaos of change. This energy boost, and the fact that we get a brief reprieve from the everyday beta mind, leaves us energy rich, balanced, and insightful.

Understanding Journey Information

Success in journeying is subjective and unique to each person. It is important not to judge your journey but to sit with what happened for you. See how it feels. See what bubbles up inside of you. What messages or meanings ring true? In a world of competition and one-upmanship, we are often frustrated if we do not have the mind-blowing, colorful, visionary journey that we expected or heard described by others. As powerful as those journeys are, they may not occur all the time for even the most polished and practiced journeyer. Journeys also do not always fit our perceived expectation of what we thought we needed or were looking for in that particular journey. Even so, in returning to ordinary reality after flowing with the journey, we often sense that what occurred was exactly what we needed, even though we didn't think so in the beginning or during the journey. Your journeys are perfect for you, whatever they may be.

To be your own shaman it is crucial that you bring your lessons and the wisdom conveyed by the Otherworlds into your real everyday life through interpretation and action. At times, your journey's meaning may be very simple and easy to understand, depending on how your helping spirits teach and deliver guidance. However, more often than not, Spirit teaches using metaphor or experiential imagery that may be difficult to understand at first. Spirits often do not teach in the clear, direct format that many school-educated westerners are used to having information presented. Like detectives, we must utilize our minds, emotions, wits, senses, and intuitions to decipher the truth. We must learn to speak the language of the spirits and our dreams. Doing so builds power as we learn to understand the messages of the Otherworlds and how those messages resonate with our soul-self. Many mystics talk about the feeling of an inner bell of truth that can be felt ringing in our solar plexus. (Recognizing this truth is a skill taught in the truth-spot exercise in chapter two and one that we encourage you to develop and hone.)

If the messages or teachings of a journey are unclear, sit with the information and the details of the journey and let them simmer within you. Journeys can be interpreted in myriad different ways, so check with your felt sense and soul-self to see if you feel the ring of truth resonate with your analysis. You may choose to journey again to the same or different helping spirits and ask for clarification. It is okay to ask your helping spirits to be patient with you and to help you understand. You may also ask to dream about the subject for clarification. Dreams and journeys are very similar and sometimes are one and the same. Before you fall asleep, state three times that you intend to dream about this subject and to remember the dream, and you may experience extraordinary results.

Remember, you are in charge of your life. It is up to you to interpret spirit information and utilize it in your life as you deem appropriate. We do not recommend that you make any major life changes based on journey information without substantial ordinary-world confirmation, plenty of time, and judicious consideration. Spirit is the guidepost, the illusion buster, and the truth revealer. You are in charge of your life and how you will best utilize journey information. You are the decision maker.

Since all journeyers are individuals, with different levels of development and life experiences, no two journey interpretations are alike, even for similar journeys. Each individual must interpret his or her own journeys based on the journey's relevance to their intention, life experiences, and spiritual experience. Bouncing journeys and interpretation ideas off others is fine as long as you remain true to your inner knowings about the journey. Others may have ideas that help with your understanding, or they may be totally off base. If you choose to share and ask for interpretation help, consider the ideas you receive, but then form your own conclusions. Just because someone else had a journey with a similar helping spirit or subject and interpreted it in a certain way, it does not mean this meaning will hold true for you. Your dream language may vary slightly from theirs.

Utilizing Journeys

Once you have learned how to journey, you will find infinite ways to use this technique for powerful healing and spiritual growth. Simply by stating your intention, you can go anywhere and do anything with the aid of your helping spirits. Even the sky is not the limit in journeying. Since we travel beyond space and time, anything is possible, so be creative and follow your intuition. This book will provide you with multitudes of journeys, but we encourage you to generate your own as well.

Some common intentions for journeys are to explore the landscapes of the Otherworlds, meet helping spirits, gain energy and personal power, receive guidance by asking questions, or request healing. Anything you feel spirit guidance would benefit is a perfect intention for your journey.

Journey Intention Suggestions

The following journeys can and should be repeated often for maximum benefit.

- Journey to each of the three worlds in separate journeys to explore the landscape. The Otherworlds are vast, infinite, and dynamic. The more you journey to them, the more you will learn.

- Journey to each of the three worlds in separate journeys to explore and experience the various energies of that world using your felt sense.

- Journey to each of the three worlds in separate journeys and utilize your different senses to experience your journey. Focus on sensing and experiencing, not just seeing. What do you feel? What do you hear? What do you smell? What do you touch? What do you see? Be aware of any knowings, intuitions, insights, and information that come to you.

- Journey regularly to each of the three worlds in separate journeys to practice journeying.

- Journey to your departure point and stay there. Explore and experience the power of this sacred place. Notice what you sense, feel, and experience. Notice yourself in that place.

- Journey to any of the three worlds to practice honing your spirit and energy connection skills.

- Journey to any of the three worlds to practice releasing any expectations or fears you may have about journeying or connecting with Spirit. Practice releasing and surrendering into the power of the journey by emptying your mind and allowing your journeys to happen.

- Journey to any of the three worlds to practice allowing yourself to go deeper into a trance and deeper into your shamanic experiences.

- Journey to any of the three worlds to take soul-filling, body-healing, mind-resting "vacations" from everyday life stress. By interrupting the cycles of worry and mind chatter, these breaks will help you see and think more clearly upon your return to ordinary reality.

- Journey to any of the three worlds to meet and connect with helping spirits.

- Journey to any of the three worlds and ask for a healing or teaching.

- Journey to any of the three worlds and ask questions about shamanism, journeying, and connecting with Spirit.

- Journey to any of the three worlds for guidance about everyday life concerns.

- Journey to any of the three worlds with your concerns, challenges, and your own intentions and questions.

- Journey in any of the three worlds and ask to open and widen the hollow bone of soul and spirit energy flowing within yourself.

- Journey in any of the three worlds for fun. Go on an adventure for power, joy, laughter, energy, or a new or different experience.

Exercise: Tree of Life

The Tree of Life exercise can be done as the visualization described below, or you can do it in a journey. If you practice it as a journey, first read the description in its entirety, then lie down and relax in your soft space, turn on the CD, and perform the exercise in your journey. As a visualization, it is especially powerful to practice the exercise outdoors, if you can, but equally effective indoors.

Begin by taking in a deep breath, closing your eyes, and relaxing for a few moments. Use the five-step process—setting an intention, focusing, releasing, allowing, and accepting—to help you perceive and receive spirit connection. Focus your attention and your intention on connecting with Otherworld energy.

Stand with your feet hip distance apart, arms down at your sides. Relax and allow yourself to slip into a light trance. Stand as solid as a tree here in the Middle World and become the Tree of Life that bridges the three worlds.

Feel the soles of your feet open to the Earth. Imagine roots growing out of the bottom of your feet, going deep into the Earth and even deeper down, into the Lower World. Feel the Earth, the many layers, temperature changes, and the texture of the soil as it changes down through the layers. Feel your roots going deep down through the water table and beyond to the core depths of the Earth and the Lower World. Breathe in deeply and feel the life-force energy of the Lower World. Feel the vibrations, pulsations, and undulations of this powerful energy. When you are ready, draw this energy up through your feet and legs into your torso, imagining your torso is the trunk of your tree. Feel the energy mingle with your tree essence here in the Middle World. It may feel tingly or warm.

Now raise your hands, palms up to the Sky, the Upper World. Imagine your arms are the branches of your tree touching the entrance into the Upper World and gathering in the life-force energy. Feel the energy of the universe and cosmos. Extend further into the Upper World and breathe in deeply. Feel the high-vibrational life-force energy of the Upper World. Feel that energy come down through your arms and head, into your trunk, and mingle and mix with your tree essence and the Lower World energy. Breathe deeply; feel deeply. Feel the vibrations, pulsations, and undulations of this powerful energy. Honor the connection.

Thank the universe for all of creation. Thank the Earth for sustaining life. Thank the Upper and Lower Worlds for sharing their wisdom and their healing and energizing powers. Thank the trees and the Middle World for bridging both the other two worlds. Feel that you are that bridge connected to all of life. Thank yourself for being that bridge. Notice how you feel. Continue the exercise for as long as you choose.

Sit quietly for a few moments and reflect on your experience. Be peaceful and thoughtful. Be present in your body and conscious mind in the moment. Express your experience, thoughts, and feelings in your journal.

Because journeying is an experiential technique, it is always a very intimate and personal experience that is unique to each and every journeyer, journeying time, and journeying space. Because each journey is personal and unique, it is difficult to fully understand the nature of personal journeying through descriptions and discussions. Journeying must be experienced firsthand, and we recommend practicing it often—daily if possible. We journey at least once per day, if not several times, and have found it to be a life-saving, life-changing, and life-empowering technique. If you truly want to be your own shaman, embark on a daily practice of journeying and watch your inner and outer worlds expand. We highly encourage you to journey often and use your felt sense to notice the effects.

We have just gotten started practicing a powerful technique that has been handed down for thousands of years. We hope you are excited about bringing energy, power, and wisdom into your everyday life through journeying. The remaining chapters will utilize the technique of journeying, along with ceremony, ritual, and specific exercises, to deeply explore the worlds of everyday life, nature, the elements, the directions, Spirit, and your own soul, psyche, and luminous energy body.

CHAPTER FOUR

Ceremony and Ritual

Ogedoda Galun'lati ogadogsi, osda nuwati Elohino, yolda hoyona, wado.
(O Great One who dwells in the Sky illuminating all that is, giving
Good Medicine of life and the Great Creation, our Mother Earth,
knowing that all the things are as they should be, we give thanks for
the beauty of all things.

—Tsalagi (Cherokee) prayer, James David
Audlin (Distant Eagle)[v]

She trembled with such power and ecstasy that she felt she might burst open and spill out all over the room in a fiery volcanic explosion. The drums pounded, moving around the inside of the circle, coming closer and closer. With a heavy sigh and the fortitude of an unyielding mountain, she held her place as they went by.

"Why don't you dance and sing?" the dragonfly questioned.

"I am afraid," she answered to the voice inside her head. "I can't sing."

"Who cares!" said the grinning, blue-winged being, now hovering directly in front of her eyes. "We know that it is all beautiful. You are beautiful! It is time you knew that too."

Before she knew what was happening, she was standing and shaking her rattle to the beat that was pounding in her head. The drummers gathered around her, and rhythmic words flowed from her mouth in beautiful song. It all seemed so strange to her, yet the power was so strong it propelled her forward into the middle of the circle. The momentum accelerated her movements into a graceful dance expressing the sacred passion of the song. The rattle seemed to take on a life of its own as it sounded out the rhythmic beats that founded the song and dance.

Around the inside of the circle she swayed and sang with an exuberance that was felt by all. Around and around she went until the energy began to dissipate, and she found her seat in the circle. Breathing heavily and grinning from ear to ear, she graciously accepted the hugs from nearby circle members.

She had never felt so full of power. She would never forget that song and rhythm. Years later, as a part of her daily spiritual ritual, she still sings and rattles it with heartfelt love and gratitude.

Ceremonies celebrate life! Ceremonies celebrate power and energy. Ceremonies celebrate rites of passage. Ceremonies celebrate Spirit and people. Ceremonies manifest the Web of Life in tangible ways that connect us to the greater whole. Ceremonies have been used by all cultures since the beginning of humanity for a whole host of different reasons and occasions. Though we still practice some ceremonies in our modern culture, much of the pomp and circumstance has been removed from our lives. This is unfortunate and may be fundamentally unhealthy. Ceremonies celebrate life, but in general, our post-industrial culture takes life for granted and does not honor its beauty and sacredness.

We are a culture that deals in statistics, acceptable losses, risk, and collateral damage. We calculate what we will accept in the numbers of dead among our neighbors and how many lives it will cost us to operate within a society that does not provide adequate healthcare for its poorest citizens. By placing limits on what we will do to help each other, by calculating the acceptable number of people who will die from a particular pharmaceutical preparation, we basically accede to a reality that says life is valuable to us only to a point. Up to that point, life matters—after that point, not so much. The ultimate extension and conclusion to this attitude is that indeed life doesn't matter within the framework of a consumer society. Commerce trumps conscience, suggesting the only thing that does matter is the economics. Our rituals have become the ceremony of acceptable cost and consumption, and we have become compliant zombies feeding off this policy of death. This culture of indifference is a direct product of our separation from the traditional involvement with life and death. The great majority of us never need to harvest a life to sustain ourselves and to feed our families; we buy animal flesh wrapped in plastic. We have become disconnected from death and therefore from life. We have abandoned our most basic rituals of life, and in so doing we have lost the richness and the depth of being alive. Ironically, as this trend progresses, we find it easier to destroy life. We cut down trees for parking lots, pollute Mother Earth, and kill each other. We can change this downward spiral by adjusting our perspective and creating ceremony of, and in, our life.

The perspective shift simply requires awareness. Pay attention to your life. Celebrate your life. Notice the richness and the beauty. Notice the pain and sadness. Don't shy away from the rich experiences of being alive. Let yourself feel them all fully and be involved up to the elbows in your life. A famous Chinese proverb says, "People in the West are always getting ready to live." It's time we start living by stepping into our awareness and saying *yes* to the joys and sorrows of life.

Take a moment now to pause and reflect upon all of the bounty and all of the beauty that is in your life, that *is* your life. Think about your loved ones and the ones who love you. Think about the things you love to do. Think about the things and places that you cherish. Think about the sadnesses that touch your heart. Think about the songs or poetry that sing your soul. Think about how special life really is, and then think about how fragile it really is. At every moment life changes. Shouldn't this fact be noticed and celebrated? Celebrated not because someday it will be too late, but because this precious moment is upon us right here, right now.

Living life in bare awareness and reverence is living every moment of your life in ceremony. It is preferable you live this way and never participate in a formal ceremony rather than attend ceremonies and not live fully in your life. Living life as a ceremony in celebration of life makes participating in formal ceremonies that much more rich. As the core elements of ceremony are described throughout this chapter, apply them to your everyday life and make each day a living ceremony.

Gateway to the Sacred

The reason that ceremony and ritual are celebratory is not only because of the event that may be the reason for the ceremony, but also because being in ceremony and ritual opens us up to the portals and gateways to Spirit. It creates an opportunity for us to shed our everyday world and open our soul to directly connect with the energies and powers of the spirit worlds and the Great Web of Life. Like journeying, which is a form of ceremony, ceremony opens the doors to the sacred and heightens our perceptions, so that we can experience the energies and powers found there.

We need ceremony and ritual to feed our soul. Too much mundane living in the world, especially without awareness and connection to Spirit, causes us to become spiritually dull and lifeless. We need to sing and dance and pray to keep ourselves fully alive and interconnected with the Web. Many people who sing shamanic songs and chants don't have performance-quality voices. But Spirit doesn't care about that. It knows they have good heart voices—that they sing from their heart and sing without embarrassment in circles and groups. There is such freedom and power in singing, dancing, and praying with wild abandon. There is no better way to tangibly experience Spirit in your body and soul.

Spirit energy in your body and soul is spirit energy here in the Middle World, where we live. We need this spirit energy to be energized, awakened, and divinely guided, so that it can heal us, others, and the world.

Ceremonies and rituals can be used for anything and everything, and they are all sacred, no matter how big or small. The simple act of saying the prayer at the beginning of this chapter with heartfelt gratitude is a sacred ceremony. Don't underestimate the power of the seemingly insignificant to affect your world.

Hundreds, if not thousands, of ceremonies and rituals have been handed down, shared, and created for every purpose under the moon and the sun. The objective of this chapter is not to teach you these ceremonies, but to teach you how to effectively create your own ceremonies and how to get the most out of your participation in ceremonies that you attend. With the increased interest in shamanism and spirituality in the West, we have been blessed with many elders, healers, and teachers of differing ancestries stepping forward to share the gifts of their teachings with the rest of the world. It would behoove us to be still and listen to their teachings and participate in their ceremonies with open hearts, minds, and souls. When we do, we will learn a lot about ceremony and a lot about ourselves.

Ceremonies and rituals are gifts from the spirits to help us connect to Spirit and to each other. These gifts are sacred. They are also abundant and freely given. Imagine how excited you might be if you were a helping spirit trying to get a person to connect with you more often, and the person came to you in a journey asking for a ceremony to become more aware. Mark Stavish, renowned alchemist and chronicler of the Western mystery tradition, says, "By the very fact that we call upon God, the archangels, the invisible ones of Creation, they are there, and in our petition, they rush to us, that we might become aware of them."[vi]

In our experience, what Stavish says has always been true, and we've found that beautiful ceremonies are created between spirits and seekers. Because the spirits can help create ceremony, there is no need to copy or imitate another's gifts. If you are going to practice ceremonies that have been given to other people or cultures, please be impeccable. Do so only when trained and given permission by a person with the authority. This integrity makes for better relations between cultures as well as more potent ceremonial experiences.

Creating Sacred Space

There are countless ways to create sacred space for your ceremony and ritual practice. Incense, sage, holy water, alcohol, words (chanted or intoned), sound (music, whistling, or bell tones), making offerings, banishing, and benediction are all things that various traditions use to lay out a ritual space. Many sects and denominations have extensive rituals that, in and of themselves, are designed to consecrate space for spiritual activity.

So how should you create a sacred space? The simplest answer is for you to use the method that works best for you. Creation is a function of intent, and it is your intention that will create the sacred in your environment or anywhere else. It is important to remember that we are all children of God, or the Web, or whatever holy source you treasure and revere. Sacred space, ritual, and ceremony are physical representations of spiritual principles or powers. Consecrating sacred space in order to represent your revered spirituality is an act of sacred creation. Therefore, your sincere and focused intention will create the climate you need for your practice. What follows is a set of suggestions that you may find useful.

Choosing a space that is to be your sanctuary may be as simple as turning an unused room into ritual space or as complex as building a temple in your back yard. It might be as simple as picking your sacred tree to sit under, or as complex as landscaping your yard with mythically symbolic trees, bushes, gardens, statuary, and a fire pit. The choice is yours, but be sure to choose and construct your space mindfully. Use your felt sense to find the right place, the perfect location, for your spiritual work. Find a location that seems to automatically drop you out of your everyday beta mind, sending you naturally deeper into your thinking machinery, into alpha or even theta. If you have a choice of more than one location in your house or apartment, choose the spot that is not overrun with foot or pet traffic. This is sacred space you are laying out here, so you are going to want a degree of privacy, or at least peace, in the space you pick.

For you to perform your ritual cleanly and clearly, full of inner peace and free of distraction, you will want to find the spot you resonate with—your power spot—and use it as a center point of your sacred space. Again, use your felt sense to locate the point within the designated space that you could categorize as yours and yours alone. There are lines of energy in and on the Earth, grids of force that map out the Earth's energy body. The Earth's surface has an energetic complexion, in other words, so some spots on the grid you will resonate with and some you will not.

Creating Your Altar

One thing we recommend, and that many people like to do as they design their sacred space, is to set up an altar. Traditionally, altars are set up in the center of a sacred space, where they become the portal or central axis to the Otherworlds. When this is not possible or desired, altars can be set up on the east end of the room or in a location to the east of your power spot, or center point. The east is the place of new beginnings, the region of potential, enlightenment, and rising power. It is an auspicious direction for spiritual work of all kinds, so facing it during ritual can be particularly advantageous. This view of the east, though, is purely subjective. It is an idea, and as with any idea, it is useful only if incorporated wholeheartedly into your belief system. It is your belief that gives the placement of your altar power. So choose the placement that works best for you and that you will be able to work with most effectively. Many people choose to align their altars along the lines of the cardinal points because doing so orients their sacred space with the greater natural world, linking the two. It is particularly advantageous to align your altar with the orientation of your personal medicine wheel, which we will discuss in chapter six. In any case, it is to your advantage to examine what it is that you believe and want to represent in physicality. What we believe is the truth of our existence. Knowing the origins and nature of that truth gives us power.

Since the altar is the focal point of many meditations, ceremonies, and rituals, you will want to set it up in such a way that it perfectly represents the spirituality best reflecting your belief. Altars can be designed to represent specific energies or to augment specific ritual ends. Indeed, esotericists design different altars for each different magical procedure. In comparison, most of the shamans we know set up their altars as multipurpose power centers; they set the altar up to represent the full spectrum of energies they resonate and work with. This setup includes representations of the elements as well as power objects, tools, and mementos from moments of peak performance or initiation. Choose an altar layout and design that empowers you.

Generally, you will choose the floor, a surface, or a tabletop to serve as your altar. Place a cloth, called the altar cloth, on top of it. This altar cloth represents the veil between the mundane and the extraordinary, the profane and the sacred. It is the barrier that will sit between your physical reality and the items you choose to represent your spirituality. The altar cloth can be made of anything, but it is to your advantage to pick a fabric that is significant to you, even if it is the remnants of an old garment you held sacred. Everything that sits on your altar should mean something to you, so choose your altar cloth mindfully.

Next, it is customary to include representations of the elements: fire, water, air, and earth. For fire, most altars employ candles. The color of the candles should reflect your nature or ritual purpose: blue or purple for action, green for a contemplative nature, red if you are a fiery or passionate type, and white if you express creativity. Gold is a universal color that represents the transcendent soul, so gold candles are often used for spiritual work.

For water, it is recommended that you have a cup or chalice in which you can keep a bit of fresh water or water from a power place, such as a waterfall, spring, river, or lake. If this is not practical, you can place a mirror as a backdrop or a platform for your altar, as mirrors represent water. Because the moon and water are so closely linked, some use lunar symbols to represent elemental water.

For air, most people use incense or feathers that they have found. For incense, pick a fragrance that suits you, or research the many uses of incense varieties on the market.

For earth, a small stone from one of your places of power will do. This representation of earth is also the first of many power objects, or power tools, you can place on your altar to enhance your effectiveness, add power to your ritual, and lend energy to your work.

Some shamans with an Eastern bent include pieces of wood to reflect that element, as described in Chinese belief, as well as a coin or some kind of ore to represent metal, another element of that system.

Power Objects

Power tools are anything that reflects, represents, is derived from, or augments your personal power. Statues representing helping spirits or ascended masters, animal totems or fetishes, signs, symbols, pictures, colors, numbers, mandalas, medicine bundles, prayer flags, rosaries, bells, gems, stones, herbs, leaves, dried flowers, shells, eggs, jewelry, mementos from peak experiences you have had or initiations you have undergone, and mementos from power spots, your personal power spot, or journey departure point are all examples of power tools you may wish to include on your altar. These are not indulgences you collect in order to create a personal museum. Rather, they are objects that sustain you, represent something that sustains you, or add energy to your life in some way. You can create them, as you do power braids and personal talismans, or you can pick them up, as you do a pebble from an energy vortex you may have visited in the American Southwest or a bit of bark from the Amazon rainforest. They can be gifts, such as family heirlooms, or gifts from the spirits, such as rocks or gems that resonate with you or a bit of shattered wood from a lightning tree. Perhaps there is something that represents who you truly are at your very best—something that, just by looking at it or holding it, brings you back to yourself. Or maybe you have something that represents an event when you were at your best or when you were pushed past your limits, yet you were sustained or you triumphed in some way. These too are power objects, as the memory of these times can enhance your performance and remind you that you are far more than meets the eye.

Power objects can be anything, really, that may cover the full spectrum of your life experience. Place these objects on your altar in a way that suits you, so that you may benefit from their presence during your spiritual moments in meditation and ritual. Depending on the nature of your ceremony or ritual, you may choose to draw on the power of specific items in order to produce a particular end or outcome. For certain healing rituals, you may hold a particular herb, as the herbalists who practice plant-spirit medicine do. Or perhaps to open your heart, you will hold a chunk of rose quartz or a ruby during your ceremony. Maybe you will draw on a statue of an elk for endurance, or one of the goddess Diana for courage, or one of Jesus as you prepare for sacrifice or rebirth. The power of the Earth, the power of your relationships and experience, and the power of your gods and helping spirits can all be present on your altar should you choose to place representations of them on it. There they will stand as partners and witnesses as you carry out your ceremony and ritual.

Creating Ceremonies and Rituals: The Three Elements

Creating and performing ceremony and ritual boils down to three universal elements. These three elements are the same for shamanic practitioners as they are for the Buddhists, Hindus, Wiccans, or Judeo-Christians. They are the holy trinity of spiritual discipline and, when properly employed, comprise the key to the kingdom. They are intent, focus and energy.

Intent is the goal, purpose, or meaning of the practice. Just as it is important for us to set our intention before we journey, it is important to set an intention for ceremony. Intent binds us to the task, focuses our energy, enables helping-spirit energies to effectively interact with us, and helps us interpret our experience.

Every ritual has an intention — the goal that is understood and the meaning that is clear as the ritual is performed. Clarity of intent is essential if we are to utilize the energies of the universe for our benefit. Nothing will come of ceremonial work without proper intent and properly stated intent.

The tricky part of intent is that we first need to know what we want and then be able to state it clearly. We need to fully understand what we are really after before we can make anything happen. In our respective healing and counseling practices, we talk with people all the time who have no idea what they want or why they want it. It's common for people to say they want more money. Sure, everybody needs more money, but it is important for them to know why. Invariably, their answer, their actual goal, is something completely different. That's why understanding and addressing our intention is so very important. We can't expect any degree of productive outcome from ceremony with inaccurate, conflicted, or undirected intent about what we desire.

Do you want inner peace, spiritual insight, or to gaze upon the face of your helping spirit or teacher? Okay, but what then? What do you plan to do with that peace, that perspective? Intent demands not only that you know what you want, but also that you fully understand the purpose of your desire, what it means to you, what changes it may bring to you, and the shift within you that will allow your manifested intent to be integrated into your life.

Words are powerful energy. When spoken in ceremony, they have even more potent power. Therefore, when formulating your intent for any ceremony, it is very important that you take plenty of time and deeply consider each word you will be using. Do the words describe your desired outcome clearly? Think about any other possible meanings for the words and statements you have designed. When creating your intention, it is always best to follow the rule of thumb, "Be careful what you ask for, you might get it."

The second element is focus. Focus is the mechanism we employ to deliver the energy we have raised to the intent we have specified. It is the means, the discipline, and the pointed action we take to set our intent in motion. During ceremony, energy is gathered, built, and concentrated through the action of focus. For a Zen Buddhist, the practice of sitting in meditation is the focus. Meditation itself isn't the intent of the practice, nor does meditation generate any energy on its own. What meditation does is focus one's awareness. The actions performed in ceremony; creating sacred space, calling to the directions, making invocations, raising power, utilizing the energies, and releasing—are all performed as acts of focus. We create our sacred space to pinpoint the area of activity and to dispel any influences that may draw energy away from our intent. We call upon the spirits in order to specify which energies we wish to manifest. All of this activity is focus.

Each and every one of these acts is a necessary aspect of focus and is extremely important to keep in mind if you are someone who designs ceremonies and rituals for your group or for your individual practice. Keep it simple. Keep it focused. The idea is to concentrate all of the energy on the intent. Unfortunately, in the attempt to make ritual interesting, we sometimes add elements for dramatic effect, but find that these elements dissipate the energy instead. We must always remember that what we focus on — what we give energy to — we give life to. Every time you direct the focus away from the desired intent, you spend some of the energy that you have raised on that digression. That digression might be fine for celebrations or feast days, when part of the intent is to spread the energy throughout the community, but it is counterproductive when you are trying to heal an illness or cocreate a new reality.

The third element is energy. Energy is everything. Energy is eternal, and energy is everywhere, all the time. The universe hangs on the energetic Web of Life. This Web exists just outside our everyday perception, and it is the omnipresent undercurrent that we draw on by setting our intent and performing our acts of focus. Energy is the fuel, the currency of the universe, and Spirit's stock in trade. We have to realize that energy comprises everything in the physical and spiritual worlds. Each thing or being has its own energetic character, to be sure, but it is energy nonetheless. We use energy to accomplish a particular task, or we direct energy in order to encourage an energetic response from a particular source.

When you come right down to it, all ceremony is the exercise of energetic sourcing — source-ery, if you will. We draw on that source energy, focusing it and concentrating it until we can release it as high-octane fuel to power our specific intent. If we have done our job properly, that energy will be enough to usher our imagined desire from the ethereal plane of concept into the physical world. Voila! We have now manifested our purpose in ceremony through the application of intent, focus, and energy.

When participating in the utilization of energy, it is important to remember that the universe is sentient. All matter is densified, high-vibration universal Web energy, and all high-vibration universal Web energy is intelligent. For this reason, we must always exercise responsibility when employing the triumvirate of intent, focus, and energy. We must also keep in mind that every component of the universe is interrelated. When we cocreate reality, we are changing the shape of the universe by redirecting and reforming the currents of intelligent energy within the Web. That great power demands great responsibility. Part of that responsibility requires being accountable for what we do. Knowing how to manipulate and focus energy doesn't mean we must feel compelled to use it compulsively. It's been said that if you carry around a hammer in your hand, everything starts to look like a nail. That self-centered view is what has brought our world to the brink. Energy, being intelligent, also has memory. When we utilize and direct energy in the service of our intent, we leave our mark upon it, like psychic fingerprints. That action is tied to us. Because of this truth, we can never perform ceremony anonymously or create a reality without accountability.

As members of a spiritual path that reveres our Mother Earth, we must employ our energetic expertise with discretion, wisdom, and responsibility. When we do, we will forever be part of the solution rather than part of the problem, no matter what our specific beliefs or practices might be. Proper ceremony will help us achieve this goal.

Content of a Ceremony or Ritual

Ceremonies and rituals have a beginning, middle, and ending in which the following actions are typically performed: creating and sanctifying sacred space, calling to the directions, invoking our helping spirits, raising power, utilizing the energies, and releasing. These actions must all be performed with concentrated focus. The more disciplined the focus, the more potent the ceremony.

Begin ceremonies and rituals by creating, sanctifying, and ceremonially rededicating your sacred space. The place where the ceremony is taking place is already alive with energy and Spirit whether it is in a building or in nature. Surrounding this ceremonial area is an even wider circle of spirits of the land and place. These spirits should be acknowledged and consulted prior to holding the ceremony. If these local helping spirits grant permission, then they should be invited to participate. If there are any spirits or energies present that do not have the highest good of the ceremony in mind, they should be directed to leave with the help of the compassionate helping spirits and a cleansing agent.

Cleansing agents remove unwanted psychic energies and debris from spaces, things, and beings. Because of the Native American influences in the West, many people are familiar with the practice of smudging—using sage, sweetgrass, or cedar for cleansing. The dried leaves and stems are put loose into a bowl or bound together in a bundle. They are set on fire, then the flames are blown out, leaving a subtle, glowing fire that causes the plants to smoke. The hands, a feather, or a wing are used to fan the smoke around, under, and over the space, object, or person to be cleansed. Other ingredients commonly used in a similar manner are incense, copal, frankincense, and myrrh. Some people use energy invoked and focused by symbols or incantations instead of, or in addition to, cleansing agents. Reiki symbols and banishing incantations are just two agents that can be used to focus energy for cleansing.

Whether uncooperative spirits or energies are present or not, it is important to cleanse the ceremonial place. Cleansing not only psychically cleans the location, but it also begins to create the sacred space for the work about to be done. As the cleansing is performed, all people present should be cleansed. They should also be prayerful and mindful of the intent to create sacred space.

Once the space has been cleansed, use intent to form an energetic circle. This circle can be created through visualization or by physically walking the circle. Some people use the smudge smoke to form the circle. The space is now prepared for ritual work.

In a large group ceremony or ritual where not all of the participants were a part of creating the sacred space, the rest of the participants can now be invited into the sacred circle. They should be directed to gather silently and reverently at a designated location, where, one by one, they will be cleansed and guided to enter into the circle. When the circle is complete, everyone should be welcomed and the ceremony begun.

Many ritual leaders like to start by holding hands and asking everyone to become fully present in their body, in the place, and in the power of the sacred circle. It is common to ask participants to notice the light of the Creator within themselves, allow it to glow and grow, move into their heart, feel it there for a moment before giving some of it to the person on their left. Participants watch and feel the light grow and glow as it moves around and around the circle. This light-passing technique is a powerful way to bring a circle together. In solo ceremonies you can use this same method to connect with your helping spirits.

Typically the next step of a ceremony is to call to and acknowledge the directions, as the next two chapters describe, and then call in any and all helping spirits, including the helping spirits of the place, land, or area, and of each participant. You may also want to appeal to other helping spirits with certain attributes, medicines, energies, or powers specific to achieving your intention. Offerings to the spirits can be given at this time. If you don't make offerings at this time, please be sure to do it at some point. It is rude and disrespectful to take without giving energy in exchange.

The middle portion of a ceremony entails power-raising in whatever form or flavor the leader, group, or solo practitioner determines will best serve the intention. Power-raising often involves drumming, rattling, singing, chanting, dancing, more spirit invocation, and prayer. The longer and more intense this activity, the more power will be raised and the greater potential for successfully manifesting the intention of the ceremony. The depth that you are able to participate and immerse yourself in during this portion of the ceremony directly correlates with the amount of energy, power, and benefit you will personally experience.

Once the power is raised, it is time to put the energy to work on behalf of the intention. It can be used in various ways depending on the ceremony and the intention. For example, if the intention of the ceremony is to heal some of the participants, these participants may be directed to sit in the center of the circle and receive energy from the participants who are filled with healing power. If the intention is to ease the pain of a war-torn country, the participants might gather in the energy and consciously propel it to that country, seeing that distant land enveloped in spiritual light.

Once the energies have been utilized, the closing begins. This may consist of a few moments of quiet, mindful prayer, drumming, or rattling followed by an expression of heartfelt gratitude to the helping spirits. In some way the spirits should be told that the work is now done. Any unreleased energies can be used to heal oneself or the Earth. Many ritual leaders like to close by holding hands and asking participants to notice the effects of the work. After a few moments of contemplation, the leader should thank everyone for participating. Sharing of the experience and food completes the closing. An offering of some of this food to the spirits is always recommended.

Every part of the ceremony and ritual should be performed with gratitude, respect, and reverence. Upon completion of any ceremony, ritual, journey, or exercise in which you have connected with helping spirits, be sure to thank them for their presence and whatever blessings, gifts, lessons, teachings, or healings they brought to you in this experience. Offerings and gifts to the spirits should be given often and from the heart.

Journeys

Journey work is a powerful way to prepare for ceremonial work. Journeys can be conducted to determine an intention for a ceremony or ritual or to clarify the wording of the intention. If you have an intention, but do not know what ceremony would best accomplish it, you may want to journey to your helping spirits and ask to be given a ceremony or ritual that will help you achieve that intention. Your helping spirits may also guide you to perform certain ceremonies and rituals in your journeys, rather than or in addition to doing them in physicality. Entering into a journey with the intention of shifting your consciousness prior to performing or attending a ceremony may help you become more deeply immersed in the ceremonial experience.

Journeys are ceremonies. Try journeying while standing and drumming, rattling, singing, dancing, and praying to make your journey even more powerful. Or add these things before or after a journey in which you are lying down.

Exercises: Three Ceremonies

The following exercises are ceremonies that should be performed with gratitude and reverence. Open up your heart, mind, and soul and immerse yourself in the sacred. Use your felt sense to perceive and receive the power and energy available to you through the practice of these ceremonies.

Begin each ceremony by drawing in a few deep breaths. Relax, and use the five-step process of setting your intention, focusing, releasing, allowing, and accepting to help you become perceptive of and receptive to Spirit connection. Drum, rattle, sing, dance, chant, and pray to help you shift consciousness. Ask your helping spirits to be with you and to help you connect with them. Focus your attention and your intention on connecting with Spirit.

Exercise One: Offerings of Gratitude

In this simple ceremony your intention is to give an offering of gratitude to the spirits for all of their help, seen and unseen. With a calm and clear state of mind and the intention of gratitude in your heart, prepare the offering. The offering can be anything that you think or have been taught that the spirits enjoy. A good rule of thumb is that spirits will likely enjoy sharing anything that you enjoy. It can be elaborate or something simple, such as a lock of your hair, a flower, some incense, a spoonful of honey, or a portion of your meal. Some people enjoy creating elaborate specific offerings, such as a painting, a special blend of essential oils, a loaf of bread, or a favorite dessert.

Once the offering is prepared, place it in a spot where the spirits can enjoy it. Under a tree, in the garden, near a loved houseplant, or on your altar are good places, but the location is up to you and your helping spirits. Talk to the spirits and let them know that this offering is for them with heartfelt thanks from you. Drumming, rattling, chanting, dancing, singing, and prayer add power to this ceremony.

Exercise Two: Helping Spirit Dance

There are many versions of the Helping Spirit Dance ceremony, each flavored by differences in tradition and culture. The form presented here is a simple ceremony that can be performed solo or in a group. The intention of the ceremony is to raise power that can be used for personal energy enhancement, healing, and increasing awareness, or for healing others.

The ceremony is performed as an active journey. Prepare yourself as you would for any journey but remain standing. Turn on the CD and/or drum or rattle. Journey to any of the three Otherworlds and meet with your helping spirits. Ask one of your helping spirits to merge with you either by you stepping into their energy field or by them stepping into your energy body. See, feel, sense, and experience your energies blending. Become filled with the energy and power of your helping spirit as much as possible.

Take on the stance of your helping spirit as you release more of yourself and relax into its energy and power. Feel what it feels like to be that spirit. If it stands, feel what it feels like to stand as it does. After a few moments, begin to move as it would, feeling its energy and power flowing through your physical body. If it crawls, then crawl, and feel what it feels like to crawl as it does. If it flies, move around as if you were flying, and feel what it feels like to fly as the spirit does. If it sits, is on all fours, or swims, do the best you can to express its movements and "dance" its energy and power. Make any sounds that it may make. Howl, hoot, or roar, flow and dance and fill with ecstasy, power, and energy.

When you are full of power or when the callback begins, stop wherever you are and absorb the energy if you are using it for personal use. Soak it in with deep breaths and conscious intent. Use your felt sense to see, feel, sense, and experience the power melting into every atom of your being.

If the intent of your ceremony is to heal another, transfer the energy and power to that person through laying on of hands and conscious intent. Use your felt sense to see, feel, sense, and experience them absorbing the energy and sinking it into every crevice of their being.

When the energy has been utilized, take in a deep breath and be still for a few moments. Soak in the energy and power of the ceremony and let it integrate. Thank your helping spirit and tell it the work is done for now. Take a few moments to notice what is happening within you and then journal your experience.

Exercise Three: Fire Ceremony

The Spirit of Fire has the power to create and destroy, which makes it a potent ally for ceremony. When this power is focused with intent, such things as difficult situations and unhealthy behaviors, mindsets, and programs can be transformed, while abundance and dreams can be manifested.

To create your own fire ceremony, determine your intent and find a safe place to have a small, contained fire. Create a talisman, a burnable representation of the thing you would like to transform or manifest. Common talismans are drawings, written words, or bundles of flowers, leaves, and twigs tied together with long grasses or yarn. You should create the talisman in silence while focusing on your intent. This silent process empowers the talisman with the energy of that which you wish to transform or manifest.

Build a fire with thanksgiving for the wood and reverence for the Spirit of Fire. Once the fire is burning, ask the Spirit of Fire to help you accomplish your intention. Invite your helping spirits to join your ceremony; drum, rattle, sing, dance, chant, or pray to build power. When the power is strong, hold the talisman in your hands and focus all of the energy of your intention upon it until it fully represents the thing you want to transform or manifest. Using mindful concentration and awareness, place the talisman in the fire and watch it burn until it is nothing but ashes. Use your felt sense and notice what you are experiencing. What shifting is taking place inside of you?

When you are finished, thank the Spirit of Fire and your helping spirits and tell them the work is done for now. Take a few moments to journal your experience.

Enjoy life, feel life, celebrate life. Live life ceremonially.

CHAPTER FIVE

Helping Spirits

*We cannot separate the physical from the spiritual,
the visible from the invisible.*

—Ted Andrews, Animal-Speak[vii]

Lying on the floor on her special blanket, she repeats the intention of her journey three times. The drumbeat carries her away to dance at the campfire of her sacred departure point in the wooded grove. The power rises in her as the dance quickens and feathers and wings transform her human body. She takes flight on the smoke of the fire and travels upwards through the blue sky, into the starlit universe and beyond. Moving through the rainbow spirals that separate the worlds in her journeys, she surfaces into a tranquil turquoise ocean. The waters are full of frolicking dolphins, smiling sea turtles, and giant whales gliding effortlessly through the watery sanctuary. Listening to their calls and feeling the vibrations pulsate throughout her body, she could feel immense energy rising within her.

Within seconds the power became so great she found herself shooting up out of the water and landing alone on a mountain plateau. An ancient master shaman appears and tells her that she is her granddaughter. Grandmother embraces her with a warm, welcoming hug that fills her whole being with an immediate understanding of this ancestor's wise and gentle essence. The soft white hide of Grandmother's dress and the smell of the herbs and smoke in her hair are deeply familiar and comforting. Her soul-self allows Grandmother's energy to merge with hers, and Grandmother communicates profound teachings of the great mysteries into her heart. She shares that she teaches in this way because the mind has great power to learn, but is also vulnerable to becoming ensnared by illusion. The heart has a greater capacity to learn, and teachings sunk into the heart and soul cannot elude us.

Grandmother and she sit at a campfire on the mountain plateau, gazing out at the surrounding peaks and valleys that seem to go on and on forever. The air is thin and clean, dusted with misty emaciated clouds, giving a surreal feeling. She breathes deeply of the life-force energy and brings it into her body. She is vaguely aware of her physical body lying on the blanket, twitching with vibrations and rapture, but she doesn't really feel it.

All too soon, the sound of the callback drumbeat enters her consciousness from a distance, and she knows she must return. After embracing Grandmother with loving gratitude, she soars down the steep mountainside, through the ocean, through the spiraling rainbow layers, through starlit universe and the clear blue sky to the smoke of the campfire. Landing in a nearby tree, she scans the landscape and then returns to the ground. In an instant, she is back in her body in her soft room, in awe of her helping spirits, the power gathered in the journey ablaze in her soul.

How much power do you think you have to change things in this world all by yourself? In recent years there has been a movement that advocates an elaborate form of wish fulfillment. This secret philosophy says that if you desire it enough, you will manifest the reality merely by holding the wish in your mind. Shamanism disputes that movement and subscribes to the position that anything of value that can be created requires collaboration. As a case in point, anyone can sit alone in their room and imagine the creation of a baby. There are a lot of things they can do while holding that thought and desire, but it's fairly certain no baby will be forthcoming unless they collaborate with someone, particularly someone fertile and of the opposite gender. The same can be said of the artist's work. The collaboration is not in the act of applying the media itself, but in the perception of those who view it and their ultimate agreement with the artist. Without that collaboration, the artist is merely an individual who thinks they have created something of value. Without the collaborative agreement with those who perceive the artist's work, the artist hasn't really done anything.

This is a harsh lesson, but an important one to consider. Just thinking something doesn't make it real. Just saying something doesn't mean it makes a difference. In order to make a difference, we have to seek out and work in collaboration. We have to establish common ground through agreement. In order to claim our shamanic power in the coming age, we must claim our power of creation through collaboration.

Shamans create reality by collaborating with both the spirit world and with their associates in the physical world. This sacred work of the shaman is accomplished through accessing the Great Web of Life for energy, healing, power, and wisdom in order to ensure the survival and wellness of the people. This is customarily done with the direction and assistance of and in collaboration with helping spirits. Without helping spirits, a shaman would not be a shaman in the traditional sense. These ambassadors of the Web work in unison with the shaman to bridge the worlds and to bring about harmony and balance within all of the worlds and their inhabitants.

There is, however, some debate about the nature of what we refer to as helping spirits. Traditional shamans view them as high-vibrational entities, residents of higher planes or nonordinary reality, which seek to assist their shamanic go-betweens with their work in this world. Some others view helping spirits as energies that shamans utilize to make a specific difference in the world, much like a chef would use different flavors to create a trademark culinary master-piece. Each energy, like each flavor, produces a specific effect on the final or desired outcome. Another view that many neo-shamans hold is that helping spirits are facets of the shaman's higher self. The sha-man calls upon the layers of their own being—those resonant in the higher realms—then uses these energies as conduits, drawing power directly from the Web to manifest change on the Earth plane.

Simple analysis of the three helping spirit models shows that they are all fundamentally speaking about the same thing. Helping spirits are energies of differing vibrations, and they manifest in different forms in order to communicate, guide, lend power, or assist in the shaman's work, be that healing, insight, awareness enhancement, or protection. It is important to realize that at the deepest levels of existence there is no separation between us and our helping spirits. Separation is an illusion. In truth, we are that which we invoke. Just as "you are what you eat," in a very real sense "you are already what you seek." It is the essence of shamanic practice to eliminate the barriers between our worlds of body, mind, and spirit in order to integrate us within ourselves, thereby drawing us into intimate harmony with all that is.

There was a time when we humans were not so separated from the natural world and the spirits as we are today. We lived directly on the Earth, in nature, honoring the cycles of all things, where we could see the interaction and manifestation of Spirit easily. This way of living is not some kind of revisionist utopian fantasy. Rather, it is the nature of an engaged life, lived close to the environment and in symbiosis with the immediate world around us. As we have hidden our natural selves, and *from* our natural selves, in the sanitized boxes of suburbia, office cubicles, congested cities, logic, reason, science, technology, and the myriad traps of modern civilization, we have segregated ourselves from nonordinary energies and perception, seemingly banishing them altogether. By abandoning the ways of living in harmony and balance with ourselves and everything around us, we have stepped away from a facet of our own humanity, and we have begun to destroy ourselves by destroying the very environment that supports us as a species. This separation of ourselves from the natural world doesn't make sense on any plane of existence, high-vibrational or otherwise. It is essentially an unnatural by-product of the complete removal of our culture and peoples from the natural world. It is antievolutionary. Being natural manifestations of the Web of Life, compassionate beings such as helping spirits are dedicated to the evolution of consciousness, and therefore to humanity because of our ability to be conscious and aware of ourselves, our world, the spirits, and the Web.

The first step in exploring our relationship with helping spirits is to understand who and what they are.

The Benefits of Connecting with Helping Spirits

No matter their name or appearance, we all have these powerful helping spirits whose "job" is to guide, protect, teach, and link us with the high-vibrational power of the Web for energy, vitality, health, and wisdom. To connect with these helping spirits, we need only become aware of their presence and allow ourselves to open and receive these precious, high-powered gifts.

Whenever we connect with our helping spirits, with whatever intention, we have the opportunity to tune into and draw in the high-vibrational energy of the spirits and the Web. Availing yourself to this energy is a powerful way to energize and heal yourself, since the connection raises your vibrational rate to be more like theirs. As your capacity to operate at higher-vibrational levels increases, you are able to fill with, hold, and utilize more and more spiritual energy and power. Doing so ignites your personal energy and activates your luminous energy body, thus giving you more energy for life. Additionally, this increase in energy repairs and heals energy-body maladies that are the cause of illness, disease, and pain.

Connecting with helping spirits has many additional benefits. Spiritual energy is conscious and intelligent and can be accessed for such things as guidance, wisdom, knowledge, elevating consciousness, improving quality of life, and creating miracles. This is not to say that spiritual energy is a panacea to save us from life's struggles. Rather, it gives us a very powerful tool for responding with strength and poise to life's challenges. During a shamanic training we attended a few years ago, someone likened the relationship between helping spirits and humans to that of participants in a sporting event. The helping spirits are on the sidelines coaching, refereeing, and cheering us on, while we are on the playing field experiencing the game's trials and triumphs. This image should remind us that we are in charge of our life, but we don't have to do it all alone. Helping spirits provide a focus and a specific representation of what we are trying to access, the traits and abilities or characteristics we are attempting to embody. When we stand firmly in our power, ask for assistance from the other realms, and engage with more than our ordinary world, we are able to live more wisely.

Our helping spirits extend us unconditional support, in part, to help us know that we are not alone and that we are not isolated inside our skin or restricted to this plane of existence. As a strand on the interconnected Web, we are intimately joined in a universal partnership with all of the energies around us. Connecting with our helping spirits on a regular basis deepens and familiarizes us with our connection with all things.

To shamans, helping spirits are not only allies, teachers, and gurus, but they are also friends, compadres, soul brothers, soul sisters, soul mates, and soul family. They are cherished companions. Oftentimes shamans spend as much or more quality time with these associates as they do with their ordinary-world friends, families, and coworkers. More than a valued friendship, the connection with spirits becomes a part of us. We also then become responsible for nurturing and maintaining this relationship. In so doing we renaturalize ourselves, bringing ourselves back into harmony with our environment and the natural order.

This special bond with our helping spirits has mutual evolutionary and enlightenment benefits for both parties and for the world. Interwoven into the fabric that provides support, guidance, and power to the shaman and well-being to the people is an elevation of consciousness and energy vibrations that helps us and our helping spirits progress in our evolutionary process. Simply put, humans and helping spirits are made from and made up of energy that is striving to become fully conscious itself. Our helping spirits know this, but most humans do not. So in addition to working in harmony with humans out of compassion for the human experience, our helping spirits also work with us to help elevate our consciousness and energy vibrations. As we evolve, this elevation creates a ripple effect, within which the helping spirits evolve, the Web evolves, the whole world evolves, along with the entirety of creation. Even the tiniest advances register energetically, and evolution occurs.

As an important function of the evolutionary process, helping spirits will generally work with us even if we are quite unaware and unenlightened, because they benefit when they help us become aware and free of illusion. Through messages that are often viewed as coincidences, synchronicities, and omens, the spirits nudge us along our path, rendering subtle assistance and often unseen, divine guidance.

As counterintuitive as it may sound, there are no such things as time and space in the spirit worlds. In a single journey, we can live entire lifetimes, or dissect a single moment, telescoping it out so that each nanosecond can be studied in minute detail. Sequential time is an illusion. All of eternity is happening simultaneously, with past, present, and future all occurring in the same instant. It is only the limited perception of the conscious beta mind that divides eternity up into tiny little pieces so that they can be discerned and observed. Because past, present, and future are occurring concurrently, it is possible through journeying to access any time or anyone in any moment in time, whether they are ancestors of the distant past or descendants who are yet to appear in the distant future. In this way, we can influence individuals in the time stream using our shamanic awareness and techniques, and they can influence us.

The spirits of our descendants are a source of great energy, information and wisdom. Just as we can journey into the past to connect with, and learn from, the spirits of our ancestors, we can journey into the future to meet with the spirits of our descendants to learn about things to come. Imagine what differences we might be able to make in our lives and in the world by looking at our now from their vantage point in the future. Perhaps with this foresight, we would make informed choices that would not only ensure the survival of our planet and her inhabitants, but our continued evolution of awareness as well. As healers, imagine what advanced technologies of healing await us in the future that we could begin using and developing now.

Spiritual Communication

Spirit speaks to us continually in our everyday life in many different ways. Shamanic traditions teach us that when an animal crosses our path, it would behoove us to study that animal. By learning about its attributes, behaviors, colors, fundamental nature, and other characteristics, we can understand messages that guide us in our own life situations or teach us about ourselves. Guiding and teaching spirits strive to help us recognize our strengths, powers, and natural talents, and they often send messages to us as signs or seeming coincidences involving animals, nature, or happenings in our day and interactions with others. It is important that you begin to pay attention with bare awareness to all of the things, significant and seemingly minor, that happen in your day. As you take notice, ask yourself what significance an occurrence has for you, and then pay attention to the answer that resonates from your felt sense and your internal wisdom.

Not paying attention to these messages is disrespectful to the spirits and disadvantageous for ourselves. When we fail to acknowledge signals or take appropriate action, we may be guided with stronger and more noticeable messages. These vary in intensity depending on individual circumstances, but often appear as challenging situations that cause us to feel uncomfortable enough to take notice and make changes. Things such as altercations with coworkers or loved ones, minor accidents, or illnesses are cosmic two-by-fours. If we ignore or miss these messages, they will come around again in stronger, more noticeable, forms. Unfortunately, it sometimes takes a hit with a bigger board for some of us to pay attention. Things such as loss of employment, divorce, car accidents, and more severe illnesses are cosmic ten-by-tens. These events are intended to be wake-up calls to help us become more present and aware in our life and on our spiritual path.

Becoming Dispirited

Sometimes helping spirits abandon a person, causing spiritual power loss. Shamanically, this abandonment is referred to as becoming dispirited. Spirit help may be lost for many reasons. If we have not honored our helping spirits, recognized them, asked for their help, or followed their guidance, they may distance themselves from us. Disregarding our destined path, misusing our power, and persistently practicing unhealthy behaviors, such as self-sabotage and substance abuse, can also cause this spirit disconnection.

When a person becomes dispirited, they experience a power deprivation in which they may feel lost, anxious, or disconnected without knowing why these feelings are occurring. Symptoms of power loss can include chronic fatigue, chronic illness, depression, anxiety, panic attacks, insecurity, vulnerability, weakness, ongoing misfortune, absent-mindedness or inability to focus, susceptibility to psychic attack and energy leakage, and other chronic problems.

Power loss may also be indicated if a person is having difficulty with their own personal journeys, meditations, or intuitive insights.

Another symptom of becoming dispirited is loss of purpose, choice, and direction in life. When this occurs, it is important that the person journey to meet with their helping spirits in order to re-connect, seek information about why the helping spirits left, and re-create a bridge from the physical world to the spirit worlds to reconnect with the lost power.

If you are feeling fatigued, tired, lost, powerless, depressed, or ill, it is time to receive a transmission of spirit energy to amplify and activate your own life force. When you are feeling good, make the connection, and this powerful energy will help you feel great!

How to Connect with Helping Spirits

Most of us have had helping spirits aiding us throughout our lives, even if we have not been consciously aware of them. One indicator of the presence of a helping spirit is a natural attraction to or an affinity for a certain thing. Perhaps you have always felt a deep affinity for angels, faeries, dolphins, horses, deer, wolves, eagles, unicorns, oak trees, gnomes, mountains, or a particular religious deity, master, or prophet. You may have collected physical representations of it, such as books, pictures, or statues. Perhaps you are frequented by certain animals or birds in your everyday life or when you travel to areas where certain animals live, such as the ocean or the mountains. These are just a few examples of ways that you have already been unconsciously connected with your helping spirits. As you become more aware and consciously deepen your connection through jour-neys and conscious intent during your everyday life, they will reveal themselves to you even more.

We all have the innate ability to effectively access the unseen; we need only retrain ourselves. As children, we all came into this world with a special gift. We had a natural spirituality, a magical creative essence that saw and believed in helping spirits and the

Otherworlds. Can you remember? Before you were trained to think with your left brain so you could fit into a rational, egocentric, technological, contemporary world, your mystical experiences were real and potent. The childlike innocence and openness that allowed you to be receptive and perceptive to Spirit back then are your tickets back to connection with the powers of the spiritual and nonordinary. It is time for you to reclaim your natural magical mysticism. As you practice the journeys and exercises throughout this book, allow the imaginative, curious child inside of you to come out to play.

In order to see, sense, feel, connect with, and utilize spirit energy, you must become open, perceptive, and receptive. Once you know who your personal helping spirits are and have made contact with them, you can call upon them directly by practicing prayer, ritual, ceremony, or invocation, or simply by asking them to connect with you. All of these methods of connection are accomplished through the bare awareness five-step process of setting your intention, focusing, releasing, allowing, and accepting.

Before you begin to connect with your helping spirits, this brief explanation of spirit protocol from the book *Energy for Life*[viii] bears repeating.

> Helping Spirits are benevolent and compassionate. They are present to help us grow and benefit from our experiences here on Earth. They are willing to help us as much as we are willing to receive that help. We may visit them for energy and health, and if we are receptive they will teach us things to help us in our daily lives. Sometimes they will present lessons that can be harsh, direct, and stingingly accurate and can leave us reeling as we process the information or experiences. Lessons of this more formidable type often occur when we didn't pay attention to the gentler more subtle ones that came first. Even as we struggle with these lessons, the Spirits hold us in loving support. The guidelines

below are "the rules" that you can count on as you connect with these high-vibrational energies:

1. All of the beings, entities or Spirits in the subtle and causal realms are benign Helping Spirits that are there to benefit you. They will not possess or co-opt you in any way against your will, and they all respect and respond to the energy protections that you will learn later in this book. If, for any reason, you feel that there is a Spirit or Spirits that are present to harm you, this is a product of your own belief system. You need to address this issue as a personal one and figure out why you want to hurt yourself.

2. Helping Spirits are honest and truthful and expect you to interact with them in like manner. If, over time, your motives for interacting with them are continually dishonest, ego-oriented, or negative they will cease to connect with and help you. They are there to give you a chance to heal and grow, not function as vehicles for wish fulfillment or self-indulgent vanities.

3. Often, Helping Spirits will speak to you in metaphor, or dream language. Their actions are representative of the message they are trying to convey to you. Images and objects refer to what they are saying and may have no meaning by themselves. For instance, a Spirit Being may take you to a waterfall and immerse you under the flowing water in order to eliminate a blockage or leak in your energy body, or to let you know that you need to do energy clearing exercises. It doesn't necessarily mean that you need to go to an actual waterfall and stand under it. Some metaphors may seem harsher than others. Maybe in the process of a journey they will wipe your face off and discard it in order to remove the false face that you wear in the world so that the real and beautiful you can shine through. We knew a shaman who for years would be asked by one of her Helping Spirits to

climb up and ride on his back, only to have him shake her off saying she was too "mucky." He did this to get her to realize that she needed to completely abstain from drinking alcohol in order to have a crystal clear high-vibrational energy field.

As you begin to explore this wonderful new energetic world, please remember that you are safe, in control, and constantly benefited by your interactions with Spirit.

Upper and Lower World Spirits

As we have discussed, there are three worlds between which shamans travel as they do their work: Upper, Lower, and Middle. Of the three, the Upper and Lower Worlds are consistently benign and predictably helpful. What follows in this section, while largely applicable to the Middle World, is completely accurate for the Upper and Lower Worlds. The Middle World, the world we live in, is unique, is a subject unto itself, and will be addressed separately later in this chapter.

Shamans understand that everything is energy—everything is made up of and made from the life-force energy of the interconnected Web. This vast omnipotent energy is a force, an intelligence, and is formless and omnipresent. It is causal energy, the highest level of vibrational energy. From a shamanic standpoint the interconnected Web is known to be alive, spirited, animated, conscious, intelligent, and divine.

Ever since human beings began to examine their conscious nature, there has been a universal need to identify this force. Philosophers, spiritual authorities, and practitioners of all kinds have long referred to it by names that imply a divine or spiritual power—names such as Great Spirit, Great Mystery, Creator, Spirit, Universal Power, Higher Power, Universal Source, the Great Web of Life, God, the Goddess, the Holy Spirit, the Lord, the Lady, Mother/Father God,

Allah, Prana, chi, ki, the Light, the Source, the Divine, and causal energy. For centuries people have argued and fought over the names, but regardless of what we call it, beyond the philosophies and dogmas is a life-force energy that lives within each of us. It is the spirit that moves in all things and imbues all things, whether observably animate or inanimate, with the spark of life. For convenience, we will refer to this energy as Great Spirit.

The all-pervading, divine life-force energy of Great Spirit has helper energies that interact with us and connect us to the subtler, pervasive life force. These energies take on particular energetic signatures and become forms we can see, sense, feel, and invoke to help us interact with them in personal and tangible ways. Some of the most resplendent energies we can interact with are the energies that coalesce into beings and forces of significant spiritual and religious importance to us. These are our helping spirits.

These spirit beings are often invisible to the untrained person because they are comprised of higher-vibrational energy and are far less dense than we are. We refer to the nature of their energy as subtle or etheric, and though the vibrations are still much higher than our own, they are more accessible than those of the very highest causal level of Great Spirit. The helping spirits exist in the energy layers of the subtle and causal—layers that are often called the spirit or etheric realms, spirit worlds, or the Otherworlds. Quite simply, helping spirits exist in the higher-vibrational spiritual aspect of our everyday world. These worlds aren't "out there"; they are right here. Because in many cases they are vibrating far too rapidly to perceive, the shaman must intentionally bridge the lower and higher energies of the visible and invisible worlds in order to have access to these nonordinary benefactors.

Helping spirits are everywhere around us, all the time, just outside of our ordinary, everyday, five-sense perception. To those who can see and sense them, they are of a lighter form than people and things—a semiform wearing a less dense cape of higher-vibrational energy. These ambassadors of the Web are as diverse and unique as the plants, animals, and humans we see in our ordinary world.

Helping spirit is an all-encompassing term under which many different forms and types of spirit energies can be defined. Depending upon our culture, in what form the helping spirits appear, or their perceived purpose, these helping spirits are commonly referred to as guardian spirits, spirit teachers, spirit healers, spirit allies, power animals, totems, spirit guides, guardian angels, gods, goddesses, ascended masters, religious deities, ancestors, or deceased loved ones. They might also be referred to as energies such as Christ consciousness, Goddess power, or nature guidance, or as archetypes with faces, bodies, shapes, forms, and names.

Like the term *helping spirits*, most of the names listed above are also broad titles used to identify a group of similar spirit energies. For example, the term *power animal* is not exclusive to four-legged, wild, furry land mammals, but also includes such helping spirits as domestic pets, birds, reptiles, amphibians, fish, insects, and water mammals. The term *ascended masters* can include religious deities, but also includes known and unknown masters of any discipline, such as artists, inventors, teachers, healers, saints, priests, priestesses, prophets, sages, yogis, gurus, hierophants, alchemists, or shamans who were once in human form on Earth. Nature is bursting with energy and spirit, and the term *nature spirit* or *elemental spirit* encompasses a great many different helping spirits. Faeries, elves, leprechauns, gnomes, the green man, forest spirits, air, fire, water, earth, plants, trees, wind, clouds, storms, sun, moon, planets, stars, and Mother Nature are powerful spirits that are often grouped together under this term. *Mythical beings* comprise a category of helping spirits that appear in mythical form, like unicorns, the winged horse Pegasus, dragons, or griffins. Helping spirits we call *angelic beings* may appear as we would typically expect an angel to look, but they may also appear as *energy beings* without form, such as radiant glowing orbs of light or color. Nature spirits such as faeries and gnomes may also appear this way.

Middle World Spirits

The Middle World is unique. It has its own nonordinary helping spirit inhabitants, but also is home to the various spirits that naturally inhabit the material world, such as spirits of place, of material objects, the organic and inorganic spirit residents of this plane, and the loitering spirits of those human beings who have died but not yet passed on to the next world. Because of this variety, shamans of nearly every tradition are very careful when journeying or working in the Middle World spirit realm. Whereas the Upper and Lower Worlds are predictably safe, because all the spirit entities residing there are working in the best interest of our world, this cannot be said of all of the resident spirits in the Middle World. Because the Middle World spirit plane overlaps the material world, and because it is widely accepted that the Middle World is the only plane in which true suffering occurs, it is necessary to be very aware, shamanically, of what is going on and exactly who and what you are talking to when working here. Many of the ordinary spirits that correspond to things that have lived or are living in the physical world can be helpful. Others can be extremely unhelpful, working in their best interest, not yours. Some tormented souls who have not passed on and who are caught in their own pain on this plane can even be aggressively unpleasant if allowed access to the energetically wounded, the weak-minded, or those that consciously or unconsciously allow them to have influence.

The spirits of natural places or those of energy vortexes or portals are neutral, being neither good nor bad. One might compare these to the natural power of lightning or water. Lightning is beautiful, but can be magnificently destructive. Water is essential for life, but too much of it, as with a flood, can be devastating. Spirits of nature are like that. Just as you would not play with a wild animal or pick up a brightly colored snake you are unfamiliar with, so too must you be careful and very respectful of many of the resident spirits in the Middle World.

To better understand Middle World spirits, it is useful to divide them into two categories: ordinary and nonordinary.

Nonordinary Middle World Spirits

Oddly enough, it is the *nonordinary* Middle World spirits that are the safest spirits on this plane. They are closest in energy configuration and temperament to those spirits we are familiar with in the Upper and Lower Worlds and are here to help us. Certain power animals, whose purpose is to guide and protect us, reside here, as do those protective spirits we call guardian spirits or angels. These spirits keep us out of harm's way, whispering in our ear at critical moments, holding us back when we are on the verge of making a mistake, or compelling us, against our better judgment, to acts of bravery and honorable commitment. These entities are our backup, and as such can be our staunchest allies and advisors.

Certain spirit teachers walk this plane, guiding us towards life lessons and helping us to interpret them through subtle inspiration. The creative Muses, those inspirational spirits familiar to artists of all stripes, work their magic here, aiding in the creation of prose, music, dance, verse, and speech. There are also spirits of insight— those that certain mediums channel during psychic readings and who advise psychically sensitive individuals as they interpret all forms of divination, such as astronomy, runes, tarot, and palmistry. These spirits are our intermediaries and couriers of this plane and work with us to manifest health and wellness in the world, providing strength when we are weak and clarity when we are pushed past resolution's power.

Some of these resident Middle World spirits were once living things that passed on to the next world, then came back to watch over loved ones or to further serve humanity and the world. It is very common for the spirits of pets to cross over, then come back to visit or linger in the home that loved and cherished them. In these instances these former pets typically and naturally protect their home and family from negative influences or other, less pleasant spiritual "squatters" that might intend to take up residence in the home.

Ordinary Middle World Spirits

As discussed, ordinary Middle World spirits are as diverse as the inhabitants of the physical world. They are the spirits of place, of nature, and of the elements. They are also the spirits of the uncrossed dead and of pain, fear, and suffering.

Nature spirits are amoral. They just *are*. They are expressions of the Web and have their own idiosyncratic characters, yet they represent the natural order. They are neither good nor bad, neither helpful nor malicious.

This cannot be said of the others, which represent a group of spirits of chaos. Shamans watch out for these spirits and are careful not to casually engage them. Because of these spirits of chaos, all Middle World journeys and any work done in this plane require vigilance and stringent attention to detail. For our purposes, we will label these two groups as natural and chaotic Middle World spirits.

Natural Middle World Spirits

Natural Middle World spirits are all around us all the time. Everything in the natural world has a spirit. In fact, everything that exists has a spirit, even inanimate objects and manmade items. Elements also have characteristic spirits. Both the elements in the earth and the representative elements of Earth and Sky have spirits.

We have spoken of the amoral character of nature. Nature is neither good nor bad—it simply is. It is the perfect, unvarnished expression of the Web of Life that we can witness in this physical plane. As such, it is at times heart-wrenchingly beautiful and in other circumstances observably brutal and frightening. Nature spirits are pure sources of life-force energy, energizing and revitalizing us. They also teach us about the impermanence of this mortality, about the forces of creation and destruction, of life and death, and of the cycles of living, dying, and rebirth. These spirits communicate at times by speaking directly to us, but more often they do so through action. Everything they do is an expression of the nature of this plane and, therefore, the nature of the universe; as such, their actions are lessons for those who pay attention. The energy found in nature is raw, primal power and exists and acts according to its fundamental character and not the prevailing social convention. Because of this, it can be gathered and applied to any purpose in line with that character. Elements are a perfect example.

Elementals

The traditional Western elements — earth, air, fire, and water — are spirits whose energies can be applied to an unlimited variety of applications. These particular nature spirits are sometimes referred to as elementals, and they are represented in folklore in a variety of ways. Sometimes they are seen as sprites, pixies, gnomes, sylphs, elves, vulcanii, salamanders, and undines (mermen and mermaids). In the final analysis, they are raw energies that reflect certain universal constants, no matter what form they may take. As their descriptions show, they reflect very natural ideas and ideals. Each has its own area of protection and application in which it excels.

Earth elementals are grounded, methodical energies that can be employed for the protection of person or property or for cultivating abundance. They are particularly helpful in gardening and similar activities. And just as planting a seed can produce fruit or vegetables, wishes or intentions tended by earth elementals can produce your own cultivated desires. Earth elementals facilitate sensation of all kinds and can therefore enhance the senses when called upon.

Water elementals help provide emotional stability and the ability to deal more openly with emotions. They are known to facilitate feeling and the fluidity of such responses within interpersonal relationships. They are useful in cultivating empathy, and because they are lunar in nature, also help us cultivate psychic gifts and talents. Folklore abounds with accounts of water elementals finding and purifying water for thirsty travelers. They are frequently petitioned to protect those who must be in or around water, such as swimmers, divers, and those on commercial or military vessels. Rainmakers and tribal shamans call upon these spirits when rain, snow, or moisture of any kind is needed, or when too much precipitation of any kind threatens the community.

Air elementals are known to protect people when traveling, whether by car, train, or plane, and there are well-documented cases of these elementals assisting those who are lost to find their way. They facilitate thinking, mental activity, and clarity. These energies are useful to anyone, but especially students of all kinds. They allow us, the curious, to understand what it is we are seeing without the clutter of our programmatic biases or self-deception.

Fire elementals are powerful transmuters and protectors during healing activities, but they are especially useful for eliminating growths, cancers, wasting diseases, and mental illnesses, such as depression. When metabolism needs a boost, fire is the one to call. The tremendous power that comes from fire elementals is very helpful in tackling all types of low, negative, or disadvantageous energies. Fire transforms, adding light and heat, and as such is thought to facilitate the use and development of intuition and insight.

Because these energies are amoral, they act as they are meant to act whether to the benefit or detriment of the one who calls upon them. For this reason, you must always pay attention to what you are doing when interacting with Middle World spirits in general. The following story illustrates this point perfectly.

A shaman we know is a well-known herbalist who makes very effective tinctures people use to cure everything from acne to AIDS. The basic ingredient in every one of these tinctures is distilled grain alcohol. Our shaman friend gathers the grapes, makes red wine, then distills the alcohol in very specific ways in order to make his effective treatments. One day he was distilling a batch in his basement laboratory. During the process, which he had performed a thousand times before, his wife called him upstairs to examine a sickly potted plant. The distillation was percolating along just fine, and since it still had a long, slow way to go, he went upstairs to examine the plant. When he looked at it, he recognized that all it needed was a little metabolism boost. He dipped into theta, called upon a fire elemental, and directed the energy to the plant. After about a minute, he heard a thunderous explosion from his basement and rushed in to investigate. He met a ball of flame rising up his basement stairs, and the house sprinkler system went off. All was brought under control, but he learned a valuable lesson that day: to pay very particular attention to what he was doing when calling upon elemental spirits. The elemental was perfectly satisfied to be directed where his thoughts sent it—into the sick plant—but some went off to his distillation, where part of his attention was occupied. He lost all the work and the majority of the lab equipment. The plant has never been better.

Resident Nature Spirits

Resident nature spirits are those that live as the nonhuman inhabitants of the world. As we have observed, everything on this plane is a spirit. Rocks, flora, fauna, wildlife, crystals, stars, planets, and even the aurora borealis all have spirit. They have not only a physical presence, but also an energetic nature. The physical presence is what they are; the energetic nature is what they do. For example, physically, the purple cone flower, also known as Echinacea, is a beautiful plant. Elegant and majestic, it stands tall in the garden, its dark central cone anchoring the lovely, needlelike petals that emanate like royal purple spokes from a wheel. Energetically, Echinacea is a healer. It helps to boost the immune system and facilitate the human body's natural defenses. It is widely used in this way, and every vitamin or health-food store in the world carries capsules and tinctures made from this wonderful plant.

So everything in the world has its own nature that can be called upon by those who know how to do it. Hematite, an iron oxide that when polished has a silver/gray, mirrorlike appearance, can be summoned to help with grounding and personal stability. Lions, the sleek and tawny denizens of the savannah, carry the spirit of strength and can be petitioned for those in need of it. The fir tree, with its fronds of lush green and its cones that open with heat and close when it rains, can be called upon to enhance self-esteem and to provide guidance, so that we more clearly define where we stand and what it is that we stand for. Mercury, the speedy little first planet in orbit around our sun, can be summoned to help us with communication, and through communication, actualization of our purpose in life.

There are two schools of thought regarding how to call upon the energies of resident nature spirits. One is to interact with the plant, animal, planet, or stone directly. Holding and rubbing a stone; eating the flesh of an animal; standing naked under the open sky while a planet is passing overhead; harvesting, processing, and ingesting a plant, as with Echinacea; or carrying a cone, as with the fir, while effective, are not necessary. Shamanically, we can journey to these entities and call upon them for assistance. The spirit and the physical are linked, but can be addressed separately. Shamanic lore is full of ways to invoke the celestial powers through ritual and the means to communicate with specific entities. Plant-spirit medicine, for example, is a branch of shamanic study that uses plant energies of the plants to heal without destroying the plant. Since most sickness has its origins in an imbalance of the energy body, energy treatment is particularly effective in staving off an illness if detected in time.

Nature Spirits of Place

Just as specific plants, trees, animals, rocks, and planets have energies that can be called upon, so do specific locations. In fact, some of the most effective energies for healing and power enhancement can be found through interacting with spirits of place. Folklore is full of references to spirits that live in or near sacred wells and springs, mountains, valleys, hills, streams, lakes, and oceans. There is an entire branch of energy work, sometimes referred to as geomancy, which studies the energy grid lines that crosshatch the globe. These ley lines and dod lines create patterns of power across the face of our planet. (It is interesting to note that nearly all of the most sacred manmade buildings in the world are built on an intersection or convergence of ley and dod lines, as are the most sacred or holy sites in history and folklore.) Where these energies meet, and even along some solitary stretches of the stronger lines, nature spirits of place can be found in abundance.

It is very common for us to stumble upon power places in nature, and these places almost universally coincide with the confluence of Earth energy. You will know them when you find them. Sitting beside a mountain lake, stumbling onto an open glade deep within the woods, standing atop a crested hill or rocky mountaintop, or resting on the floor of a valley, nestled in the arms of stone that surround you, your soul will sing in harmony with the soul song of the place and the Earth. You will resonate with these locations, and they will feed your very being, even across time and distance when you merely think of them.

Energy vortexes, such as Airport Mesa and Bell Rock in Sedona, Arizona, have very specific energies and spirits. They are so powerful and so much larger than we frail humans, they actually increase our vibrational level as we stand or sit within their sphere of influence. These spirits represent an unseen reality of such power and enormity that the effect they have on us is like a wind blowing the cobwebs out of our soul. They communicate not with words, but with action and a very effective *do* that moves and balances us, in spite of our will or personal choice in the moment.

Sacred places are home to all manner of spirits and may claim multiple entities from different times. Chartres Cathedral in France (built on a ley-dod convergence), was originally a Druid meeting place and is now a bastion of Christianity. The pyramids at Giza, the Mount of Olives, the Taj Mahal, the Vatican, even Plymouth Rock all have a characteristic spirit of place that can be moving beyond words and that can heal and edify us.

There are tales of shamans undergoing great and perilous treks to get to such power spots in order to summon the resident spirits there for wisdom, healing, insight, power, and change. Often in the tales, the shaman must have great presence of mind and be the embodiment of purpose in order to survive the interaction. The power of these entities is overwhelming and the scope of their understanding so vastly beyond the potential of their petitioners that without a singular purity of purpose, the shaman would have succumbed to the rigors of the energetic dialog. Sometimes these places are used to test the would-be shaman and are the gauntlet these seekers of knowledge and power must pass through if they are to serve their people with impeccability. Presence of mind and attention to detail is a life-or-death requirement in these stories. In the end, the shaman invariably triumphs for himself and his people, gaining the power and gifts the resident spirit can bestow. Such is the way with all neutral spirits.

Unfortunately, neutral spirits aren't all that is out there.

Chaotic or Unhelpful Spirits of the Middle World

Another group of spirits that makes the Middle World a tricky place are chaotic or unhelpful spirits. You might refer to this group as non-advantageous, because that phrasing represents less of a dichotomy. We divide these spirits into two categories, organic and inorganic.

Organic spirits that are considered unhelpful are nearly always the spirits of the dead who have not crossed over. Some of these spirits are suffering terribly. They exist on this plane because they were compelled to stay for various reasons. Perhaps they were murdered or committed suicide; perhaps they did something for which they could not forgive themselves. Sometimes they are in such pain, they cannot rest. In these cases, they can become violent or attempt to possess living human beings. They attach themselves to the living in order to try to assuage their torment, find a way out of their misery, or tell their story.

Others that have refused to cross over are just unpleasant. Many of these spirits manifest the same traits dead as they did when they were alive. If they were angry and bitter in life, they remain angry and bitter in death. If they were violent or abusive when in the flesh, they are likely to be just as vile and pernicious out of it. They cannot hurt us unless we allow them a way to influence us, but they are not unerringly honest, as are the helping spirits of the three worlds. They are serving their own agenda, and as such, will deceive those who interact with them in pursuit of their desires.

It is very common for the malicious spirits of the dead that have not crossed over to attach themselves, possess, or "piggyback" the living. When this happens, it is usually the product of some imbalance or energy leakage in the living person. When a living person has experienced a trauma or is leaking energy, they appear "cracked" or visible to the chaotic spirits. Like a predator following a blood trail, these spirits find and attach themselves to the living. Once possessed in this way, the living person can manifest all kinds of symptoms. Substance abuse, from mild to raging addiction, is a common symptom. The individual also frequently experiences the onset of mental illness. Mild neuroses to full-blown delusional schizophrenia have been attributed to attachments or possessions by the spirits of malicious or tormented individuals who would not cross over. We heard of one shaman in Brazil who, with the permission of the Brazilian government, performed depossession rituals on inmates of a state mental institution. After the ritual, fully 40 percent of those treated exhibited no further pathology and, after a period of observation, were released.

The following is the recollection of a participant in a depossession ritual performed at a workshop led by Michael Harner and facilitated by one of his shamanic students acting as medium.

The entire class was in attendance—probably sixty of us shamanic students total. The man who was the client told his story first. He had been in a terrible car accident, in a coma for a few days, and in the hospital for quite a while during convalescence. He reported that ever since he had come out of the coma, he craved alcohol, specifically red wine, like Chianti. Not having been much of a drinker before, he thought this odd, but nothing more. When he was released, he began to drink in earnest and experienced a steady deterioration of his life due to the addiction. He found himself overeating and overdrinking. He put on weight and even ended up turning into quite the philanderer. This led to the demise of his marriage and the estrangement of his children. There were times he felt his mind was not his own. He seemed to be standing next to himself when he would be doing something—almost as if he were watching himself live his own life. He had been in rehab to no avail. He could not move past the bottle or this lifestyle that was consuming him, so he had finally come to ask this group of shamans to help free him of this problem.

Michael (Harner) had his student act as medium and attempt to communicate with the possessing spirit. The main group drummed and rattled as the medium went into a trance and reached out to make contact with the spirit. The lights were dimmed, but we could all still see through the gloom. At one point Michael held up his hand, signaling us to be quiet. He asked the spirit to identify itself. At that point the student, a middle-aged woman, spoke with a man's voice. She said her name was Giuseppe. Michael then proceeded to ask a series of questions and get the full story. Giuseppe had died not long ago in the hospital—the same hospital in which the man was comatose. He had been an Italian baker who had lived a long and very happy life. He loved life so much that he had decided to stay. When he had come across the man after the accident, he had decided to live a little more. Michael spoke with him and argued a bit with him about giving up the man's body and moving on. In the end, Giuseppe agreed to cross over, and the medium, along with Michael, psychopomped him into the light and the next world. Psychopomp is a shamanic method for help-ing spirits cross over. After the ritual, the man wept and said he no longer had the craving for food and drink he had lived with for so long. Years later, we heard from him, and he was doing great, was remarried, and had not had a drink since that night at the workshop.

We will discuss imbalances and leakages further in chapter eight.

The other group of unhelpful spirits is called inorganics. Basically, these spirits are residents of this plane, but have never been alive in the conventional sense. Some are simple creatures, called larvae, and are energy leaches that can attach themselves to the living, bleeding off their energy or perhaps soaking up energy that may already be leaking from the person. Others are more complicated. They are self-determinate in their own right and are chameleons, reflect-ing the belief and demeanor of those they encounter. If a fearful person encounters them, these inorganics will appear as exactly what that person fears. Entities perceived in demon sightings are most certainly these inorganics appearing exactly as what they are expected to be—big and scary and powerful. Oddly enough, the beings perceived in many angel sightings are inorganics as well. These observers obviously have joy and love in their hearts, so the inorganics reflect that back. It is important to note, however, that both of these inorganics use the encounter to feed off the emotions and energy of the living. Fear or joy makes no difference to them. They're just hungry for energy.

Interacting With Middle World Spirits

Properly engaged, all inorganics can be used by shamans to gather information or perform certain tasks. In other words, they can be commanded by the living if commanded properly. Shamanically, they are then referred to as allies. We recommend that no shaman attempt to co-opt an ally unless they have had specific and detailed training in this practice, because inorganics can be unpredictable and even dangerous.

The truth is, the reason these spirits, whether organic or inorganic, are less than helpful is largely because the people who interact with them are not careful enough or not prepared well enough to take responsibility for the course the interaction takes. Myth, legend, and folktales abound about such entities. Demons, genies, the undead, the sidhe, and all manner of unfriendly creatures pepper such tales. The moral of all of these stories is that when you interact with spirits of this type, you need to be careful and prepared. Because we are more interested in preparing and protecting our readers than teaching mastery over Middle World spirits, we focus more on the protective aspects of shamanism. The following can be looked at as general guidelines for interacting with Middle World spirits.

The first thing to do is be careful. An ounce of prevention is worth a pound of cure. When speaking with Middle World spirits, ask many questions and employ your truth spot as described in chapter two. These spirits cannot hurt you unless you allow them to, plain and simple. If something does not feel right, or you know you are being lied to, command them, in the name of whatever higher authority you believe in, to leave. It is important that you command them with authority through belief. You can't rely on what you don't believe in to do the trick. For instance, if you are a God-fearing Christian, believing that Jesus Christ is your personal savior, then you will be able to dismiss any spirit just by commanding it to leave in his name. If you are a devotee of the Morrigan in the Wiccan tradition and you try to banish spirits using the name of Christ, it just won't work. Stick with what you believe in. If you are a true believer, the Morrigan will do the trick.

No matter what, stay neutral. Don't be full of fear, don't try to radiate love and kindness, just stay neutral. Faced with your neutrality, the beings are likely to appear as they are, rather than as you would make them. Inorganics may seem creepy because they are different forms, but they are just being what they are. Respect that. Many of these entities have secrets to share and lessons to teach. You must always carefully evaluate these lessons before employing them, but that is why you have learned to pay attention and to develop your personal discernment. Your internal feeling senses will guide you safely.

If you get yourself into trouble or out of your depth, you can always call upon your helping spirits from any of the three worlds to come to your assistance. These helping spirits are your backup if you find yourself in a situation that may be less than advantageous. They are your touchstones and, as such, can be used not only for protection, but also as confirmation of your own discernment. If you are being deceived, they will verify that. And, with a word from you, your helping spirits will take care of any problems with chaotic or unhelpful spirits you may encounter.

If you have been exposed to any kind of energy-sucking entity, or if you feel you may have picked up an attachment or perhaps an energetic spirit larvae that is feeding on your energy, use energy-cleansing methods to clear yourself. We will present these in detail in chapter eight. In fact, whenever you do Middle World work, it may be in your best interest to do a quick energy cleanse when you come out of the journey, just in case. Not only will this cleanse keep you free of attachments and energetic intrusions, but it also will help to revitalize and balance your energy field. Energy cleansing has all kinds of benefits. Use it often.

When it comes to Middle World spirits, whether natural or unnatural, helpful or unhelpful, organic or inorganic, remember this one thing: You are the one in the body. You are the one who is fully alive, fully incarnated, and fully in control on this plane. No spirit entity can assail your sovereign humanity. If anything tries, now you have the tools to deal with it.

Journeys

The following journeys can and should be repeated often for maximum benefit. State your intention to journey to any of the three worlds (unless specified), meet with your helping spirits, and do the journey described. Be sure to humbly and reverently ask for the wisdom, teaching, learning, and healing that you are seeking in your journeys.

Journey to each of the three worlds in separate journeys to meet with your helping spirits—repeat many times to meet all the helping spirits that work with you.

Journey to each of the three worlds in separate journeys, meet with your helping spirits and develop a relationship with them.

Journey to each of the three worlds in separate journeys, meet with your helping spirits and connect with their attributes, characteristics, powers, medicines, wisdom, teachings, and high-vibrational energies.

- Journey to each of the three worlds in separate journeys, meet with your helping spirits, and ask for a healing, a teaching, guidance, or words of wisdom.

- Ask to meet with the spirit(s) of your ancestors. Learn about them. Ask for a teaching or healing.

- Ask to meet with the spirit(s) of your ancestors to learn a ceremony or ritual.

- Ask to meet with the spirit(s) of your descendants to learn about the coming age and what needs to be done now to assist in any transitions.

- Ask to learn about the elements and how to use their energy, power, and medicine for healing.

- Meet with, learn about, and connect with the spirit and energies of plants. Ask how you can utilize these powers and what you can do for them.

- Meet with, learn about, and connect with the spirit and energies of nature tenders—spirit beings known by such names as faeries, greenmen, gnomes, elves, and pixies. Ask how you can use these powers and what you can do for them.

- Journey to a power place and connect with the spirits of place, such as guardians of the place and spirits and energies of the land and water. Ask how you can utilize these powers and what you can do for them.

- Meet with, learn about, and connect with the spirit and energies of a rock, stone, or crystal. Ask how you can utilize these powers and what you can do for them.

- Meet with, learn about, and connect with the spirit and energies of the nature spirits in the cosmos, such as the planets, sun, moon, stars, galaxies, and wormholes. Ask how you can utilize these powers and what you can do for them.

- Journey to the nature spirits and ask to be given a simple ritual for giving thanks.

- Meet with your helping spirits to learn about chaotic spirits and how to take care of yourself, should you have the need or occasion to encounter them.

Exercises: Connecting With Helping Spirits

Begin each exercise by taking in a deep breath, closing your eyes, and relaxing for a few moments. Use the five-step process of setting your intention, focusing, releasing, allowing, and accepting to help you become perceptive and receptive to spirit connections. Ask your helping spirits to be with you and to help you connect with them. Focus your attention and your intention on connecting with Spirit.

Exercise One: Meet Helping Spirits

You can connect with helping spirits anytime, anywhere, simply by becoming perceptive and receptive. This exercise will give you some experience in opening this doorway. In this exercise you will invite your helping spirit to come and meet with you wherever you are at that moment.

Begin by taking in a deep breath. Exhale and relax. Relax your shoulders and your neck. Close your eyes. Release your everyday thoughts and doings. Take in another deep breath, exhale, and relax. Feel your mind become quiet and your whole self become calm and peaceful. Focus your attention and your intention on connecting with Spirit.

When you feel relaxed, invite a helping spirit to come and sit with you. Be open and receptive to who or whatever appears. Use all of your senses to experience the presence of your helping spirit. You may not be able to "see" them, so notice what you are feeling, experiencing, and sensing with all of your senses. If it feels appropriate to you, when you have connected with your helping spirit, ask for a personal teaching—some words of guidance, wisdom, or a healing. Open your mind and soul, and receive this gift with your heart.

Helping spirits emit energy that resonates in our own energy body. Feel the high vibrational energy that comprises them. Notice how your energy feels when you are in the presence of their energy. Can you see, sense, or feel their brilliant energy glowing before you? Check in with yourself. Do you notice your energy body "light up" as you experience the high-vibrational energy that emanates from this spirit? See, sense, feel, and experience all the ways that your energy body changes in the presence of your helping spirits. Ask them to let you see, feel, sense, and experience their energy so that you can recognize their energy, aspects, nuances, patterns, vibrations, sound, color, and what form they take, if any. Ask them to tell you about their energetic qualities and attributes. Listen with your heart. Don't worry if it feels like you are making up your observations; it often feels that way at first. Remain open and accepting of whatever comes to you.

When you are finished with the exercise, thank your helping spirit for sharing its presence and energy with you. Maintain the energy flow as you go about your daily life.

You have many helping spirits. We recommend practicing this exercise often to meet all of them and to strengthen your spirit relationships.

Exercise Two: Circle of Power and Love

In this exercise you will be asking your helping spirits to form a circle around you to share some of their power and love with you. You can do this by inviting the spirits to be with you where you are right now, or you can go on a mini Middle World journey to your departure point or a sacred place where you would like to meet with your helping spirits.

Take in a deep breath, exhale, and relax. Relax your body and mind. Release your everyday thoughts and concerns. Take in another deep breath, exhale, and relax. Feel your mind become quiet and your whole self become calm and peaceful. If you choose to travel to your departure point or a sacred place, go there now.

Relax, and use the five-step process to help you become perceptive and receptive to Spirit connection. Ask your helping spirits to be with you and to help you connect with them. Notice as, one by one, your helping spirits gather around you. Soon you are in the center of a circle comprised of your helping spirits. You may not be able to "see" this circle so use your felt sense to feel, sense, and experience this circle of power surrounding you. Notice that your helping spirits are filled with compassion and the desire to lend support for your life journey and spiritual path. Feel, sense, and experience all of your helping spirits radiating love and luminous light to you from their centers, their hearts, and their whole beings. Allow yourself to open up and receive this mystical gift.

Soak it all in, as much as you can. Feel the power of the love and the luminescence coming from your helping spirits grow and intensify within you as they continually send the energy to you. Feel your body totally relax. All tightness, tension, discomfort, and pain leaves your body now. Notice any unhealthy energy, blockages, congestion, or false walls or masks dissolving. Feel the powerful energy saturating every cell of your entire body and then spreading beyond your physical body into your luminous energy body. See, feel, sense, and experience the energy glowing throughout your body and energy field. Your energy body, now full of power, love, and light, expands out and occupies all of the space inside the circle formed by your helping spirits. The edge of your energy body that forms your energy boundary is electrified and fortified by your helping spirits. See, feel, sense, and experience. Observe yourself, your body, your thoughts, your emotions, your soul, your energy body, and your energy boundary. Notice everything. Do this for as long as you have time.

When you need to return to your everyday activities, thank your helping spirits with deep, heartfelt gratitude for their presence and their gifts and say goodbye for now. Do your best to remain open and allow the energy to flow throughout your physical and energy bodies.

After this exercise, as you go about your day, stop periodically and notice how you feel. Do you feel power filled? Do you feel loved? Do you feel strong? Do you feel energized?

Exercise Three: Fill with Spiritual Power

This exercise entails inviting a helping spirit of your choice to be present inside your body and energy field. This direct connection with the spirit stimulates you to vibrate at its high-vibrational frequency, creating an incredibly energizing and enlightening experience.

Begin by taking in a deep breath, closing your eyes, and relaxing for a moment. Set your intention to connect with Spirit.

When you are ready, mindfully bring your awareness to your center and go deep within to your soul-self. Ask the helping spirit of your choice to come and be with you. Acknowledge its presence. See, sense, and feel it standing before you. Be aware and use all of your senses to experience the helping spirit with you. Notice all of its attributes, including its shape, size, color, and characteristics.

Ask the helping spirit if it would step inside your energy field so that you can experience its energy. See, sense, and feel it standing and directing in front of you, lined up chakra to chakra. When you feel yourselves fully lined up, allow the merging to take place. Open up your energy boundary using your intention and feel the helping spirit step into your energy field. See, sense, feel, and experience its energies blending with you. Sit quietly and feel its presence and power. Experience yourself filling with dynamic, high-frequency energy. Sense, see, feel, experience, and receive for as long as you have time.

When you are ready to disengage, thank your helping spirit and feel it totally separating from you as it steps out of your energy field. Remain silent for a few moments and notice everything that you sense and feel. Do you find that you can still feel the powerful energetic signature left behind by the energy of the helping spirit? Feel the increase in your energy and maintain that energy flow as you go about your daily life.

Exercise Four: Blend with Spirit

This exercise is similar to the Fill with Spiritual Power exercise, but includes a twist. In the Fill with Spiritual Power exercise, you are inviting a helping spirit to come into your energy field. In this exercise, you are stepping into the energy field of the helping spirit of your choice and feeling its high-vibrational energy. This exercise will undeniably raise your vibrations and energy levels. If you are interested in spiritual growth and enlightenment, this exercise will also help you progress along your path by enabling you to directly experience the higher-vibrational energies of Spirit.

Choose a helping spirit that you would like to merge with energetically. Take in a deep breath and relax. Study a picture or object representation of the helping spirit that you have chosen. If you don't have a picture or object, or prefer to connect through your own image, close your eyes and picture the spirit form as clearly as possible in your mind's eye. Focus your attention and your intention on connecting with this helping spirit. Invite the helping spirit to come and stand before you. Use all of your senses to really manifest its presence by seeing it, sensing it, and feeling it. It should be huge and towering before you. Amplify all the particulars of the helping spirit. Notice all of its attributes—shape, size, color, posture, garments, characteristics, and so on. The energy should be palpable to your felt sense.

Ask the helping spirit for permission to enter its energy field, and when it grants permission, take one step forward and enter the helping spirit.

Inhabit the helping spirit completely. Speak the name or the form of the helping spirit out loud and feel the vibration of the sound. Repeat it three times, while you see, sense, feel, and experience yourself enveloped in the energy field of the helping spirit. Sense yourself fully blended with the helping spirit. Assume its stance, posture, expression, and any other nuance about it you can discern. Allow yourself to feel its energy, to be its energy, and to feel what it is like to be that helping spirit. Relax and take your time. Allow yourself to feel its consciousness and to be its consciousness. Completely merge and blend energetically with the helping spirit. Allow it to feel your energy and consciousness. As completely as possible, be that helping spirit.

When you are ready to disengage, take one step backwards and separate yourself from the helping spirit. See and feel yourself as a separate entity. See the helping spirit towering before you and then slowly disappearing. Thank the helping spirit and bid it farewell for now.

Remain silent for a few moments and notice everything that you are sensing, feeling, and experiencing. Do you find that you can still feel the powerful energetic signature left behind by the energy of the helping spirit? Maintain this energy flow as you go about your daily life.

CHAPTER SIX

Personal Medicine Wheels— Your Circle of Power

Energy, energy circling around
Energy, energy spiraling around
Energy, energy cycling around
Around, around, around, around

Power, power circling around
Power, power spiraling around
Power, power cycling around
Around, around, around, around

Light, light circling around
Light, light spiraling around
Light, light cycling around
Around, around, around, around

—Power song gifted to Colleen by the helping spirits

She was deep in trance yet couldn't leave her departure point to travel to the Upper World as she intended. This had never happened to her before, so she wasn't sure what to do. Confused and slightly frustrated, she took a deep breath and surrendered into the process, to the quiet stillness of her sacred place. She asked what she needed to do. Great-grandfather, a trusted helping spirit that always appeared in the Upper World, materialized out of the trunk of a nearby walnut tree.

"Invite us to your world," he said kindly.

Half as a question, half as a statement, she responded, "Come here?"

And before she could finish thinking the words, all of her Upper World helping spirits formed a circle, descended through the layers, and surrounded her. Simultaneously, her Lower World helping spirits ascended and joined the circle of power. She felt reverent awe that the all-powerful beings she traveled to for teachings and healings were right here around her! She took in a deep breath and waited with anticipation for what might unfold.

At first there was no talking, but her departure point was no longer quiet or still. A distinct hum resonated through-out the forest and pulled her into its vibration. She noticed that she felt like she was buzzing; the sensation was similar to being intoxicated yet very different. She melted into the experience and let the waves of energy absorb into her body and soul.

After what seemed like hours, Great-grandfather kissed her eyes open. She felt so calm, so peaceful, and so full—full of light, full of love, full of energy. Little sparkles of light danced before her like stars in the mountain wilderness on a new-moon night. She wondered, and Great-grandfather confirmed, "You are seeing a glimpse of the Great Web. The energy you feel is a mere fraction of its power and limitless potential.

"This wheel," he said with a sweeping motion of his hand, "is your gateway to great mysteries and great powers. Build a medicine wheel in your backyard to create a vortex, an energetic connector that makes it easier for us to come and help you with your work. Spend time in your wheel, in all of the directions, and notice that you live in the center of the great wheel of life. Know that, honor that, live that way."

Tired of feeling empty and unfulfilled? Connect to your circle of power! Sick of living in pain, discomfort, and dis-ease? Tap into the energy of your circle of power! Longing for a life that is rich in beauty and meaning? Draw in the energy of the circles around you! Concerned about these tough times and the times to come and want to make a difference? Call upon the super crew of your personal medicine wheel!

One of the great tragedies of post-modern life is that people feel they are or must be alone. The shape our reality has taken allows a person to sit in the dark, staring at a computer screen or in front of the television, feeling they are in contact with the world, yet never interacting, face-to-face, with a living, breathing human being or the organic lushness of nature on any level. The upshot of this reality is that one day they wake up and realize they have isolated themselves and wasted years of their lives living within an illusion.

Shamans ask the question, "How much time do you have to waste?" Then they encourage us to reconnect, to get out from behind our mask and interact with the world, becoming engaged with the circles that are everywhere around us and within us.

Within life there are many circles within circles within circles. Your life, and all of life, is a circle. The foundation of our existence is a natural world that operates in circles. The Earth is a circle that orbits the circular sun in a circular pattern, thus creating sunrise and sunset circles. Birds build their nests in circles and lay circular eggs.

Flowers bloom in a circular display of petals surrounding a circular center. The building block of life is the circular atom, made up of even smaller circular particles. Atoms combine to form circular molecules, which combine to form circular cells, making our bodies a huge conglomeration of circles. The intelligence of our cells, our DNA, is a circular spiral. Our life cycles are circles. We have different circles of people around us— friends, families, coworkers, and neighbors—who all have their different circles. Helping spirits form circles around us to connect us to the circle of the Great Web of Life.

Circles have no beginning, no middle, and no end—they are a constant flow of life-force energy. Circles are energy in motion, and this is power.

Your Personal Circle of Power

Becoming aware of the circles of power that are within you and that surround you is vital to you becoming your own shaman. These circles are your power sources, resources, your toolbox, your shamanic bag of tricks. You have a personal medicine wheel within and around you right now, just outside of your awareness. Your wheel is a circle of power that connects you to all of the other circles within circles within circles of the Web. It is a tangible microcosm of the universe that you can see, feel, sense, experience, and utilize. With awareness, focus, and intent, you can access this circle of power for anything and everything, including energy, health, and wisdom.

Your circle of power exists in both the ordinary physical world and the nonordinary spirit world. Because most people have not developed the skills that make it possible to observe their circle with everyday awareness, it seems veiled, invisible, nonexistent, or "out there." But in reality, it is right here, right now, and you are in the center of your circle of power all day, every day.

To access your circle you will need to embark on an exploratory mission to discover the many different energies and powers that comprise your circle. Because your circle probably seems invisible or "out there somewhere" right now, you will first need to use your shamanic skill of journeying to access it. Your circle of power consists of many different powerful elements and thus requires many journeys to explore. In the circle itself, and in each of the directions, you will find numerous energies, powers, and medicines, such as helping spirits, colors, chakra affiliations, sounds, vibrations, seasons, elements, attributes, cycles, plants, and minerals, to name a few. Just as you are unique, your circle of power is unique and will be different from anyone else's.

The second part of accessing your circle is grounding the energies in ordinary reality. You ground these energies by bringing them into physical existence in one of many ways. You can follow some of the "old ways" or create your own new ways.

Creating earthly circles is a powerful "old way" to connect with your circle of power. Throughout history, humans of all cultures have honored the sacred by making physical representations of their circles, such as stone rings, medicine wheels, mounds, pits, and labyrinths. Pottery, clothing, tools, and sacred objects bear patterns and symbols of circles and spirals. Mandalas, sand paintings, pictographs, and petroglyphs tell stories and draw us deep into the universe through circles.

Earthly circles of power are made to honor and manifest spiritual energy and power for daily use. Circles can be used for ceremonies, celebrations, healings, journeys, and meditations, to give just a few examples. Some circles are created to honor and utilize the special energy of sacred or high-vibrational places. Some circles are made to form a vortex of energy and thus make a space sacred. Some circles are created as beautiful artworks or ceremonial tools. Circles focus and concentrate energy into a specific area, thus forming a vortex that can be used for a specific intention. These kinds of earthly circles are cocreated by people and Spirit.

Helping spirits teach us that they give us circles of power to help us connect. Our physical representations of these circles are gifts from us to the spirits to show them that we are thankful. Creating circles is a beautiful way for us to honor them and our connection to them.

In your explorations you may come across traditions that already have specific circles of power or medicine wheels in place. These circles vary greatly by culture. As people from these cultures teach and share their beliefs and practices, we have access to many sacred medicine wheels. You may feel drawn to some of these practices, and if so, we encourage you to incorporate their teachings into your own personal exploration of your unique circle of power.

Throughout the course of history, the world has been opening up, and people and cultures are coming together to work for the good of the world. As races and cultures commingle, teaching and learning from one another, sharing blood and lineage through multicultural marriages and births, we are becoming a rainbow race of people. This evolution will help to bring about peace and harmony. The more we know and understand about each other, the less fear there will be, and tolerance and even acceptance will result.

In the meantime, this shift is creating some interesting situations on the planet as well as in our lives and spiritual paths. Most of us are already an eclectic blend of different cultural ancestries and heritages, each with its own practices and beliefs. Yet we may find it difficult or unfulfilling to follow the spiritual path of our own cultures because it lacks depth, it has become dispirited, or we don't agree with or resonate with the path's practices, beliefs, or rules. So we look to other cultures and traditions to find the spiritual depth and connection we are yearning for. Though we might derive great value from these paths, we may also find it difficult to fully embrace them if we are not of that particular cultural heritage or belief structure. Without a fulfilling spiritual path, many people are experiencing spiritual disconnection. In our healing practices and workshops people commonly discuss their feelings of disappointment and emptiness, and their yearning to have a spiritual connection that has depth and substance. Each person's circle of power offers this connection and much more.

Accessing your circle of power is a potent way to satisfy spiritual hunger because it feeds your soul. Whether you are following no path, a particular tradition, an eclectic path, or a path of your own, connecting with your circle of power will give you the feeling of finally being home. It allows you to experience yourself as a part of the divine rather than separate. At the microcosmic level, the individual beings, energies, and powers of your circle resonate with your energy and soul. When asked, they will share their power with you and teach you how to utilize it for energy, health, awareness, harmony, wisdom, and enlightenment. At the macrocosmic level, your circle spirals out into infinity, connecting with other circles within circles, operating as your sacred conduit of the Web. If you are open to receiving this energy, this natural phenomenon acts as your direct intravenous line to divinity and infinite possibilities.

The Nine Directions

The number of acknowledged directions and the powers associated with them vary widely across traditions and cultures. Some cultures honor and address the four cardinal directions of east, south, west, and north. Some also honor and address the directions of above and below. In addition to these six directions, we feel it is important to honor and acknowledge the directions of center, circle, and within.

Traditions worldwide stress that center is a power spot in and of itself. People are the center of their lives and the great wheel of life and thus should honor and acknowledge themselves as a part of their circle of power.

People are also spirits—divine energy in human form. We are all connected. The direction of circle signifies this connection. In our personal medicine wheel, circle is also the grid of power that ties our wheel together. Each point defines a power spot on the circle, and if you connect all the points, including above and below, you actually construct a sphere of power. The points represent where the spokes connect, center defines the hub, and circle defines the rim or, more expansively, the surface of the sphere. Circle is the contact point with the outside world, where we find protection and where our energy membrane receives healing from without and from whence we deliver healing from within.

By acknowledging the direction of within, we honor our spirit energy and the light of the Creator within us. Within truly connects us to the Web and, through the Web, to all that is. Nothing is separate, everything is one. Within, as it taps into the transcendent All, honors the holistic nature of all that is.

The following list of directional attributes from a personal medicine wheel gives examples of the energies and powers you may find in yours. Remember, you are unique, and your personal wheel is unique; therefore, many, some, or none of these attributes may ring true for you. Honor yourself and your unique wheel of power by following the guidance that you receive in your personal explorations. Some attributes may belong in more than one direction. That's okay—there are no rules. Each direction will also have personal helping spirits, energies, and powers, such as power animals, plants, or crystals that are not listed here.

Center: The center of your circle is you—yourself in your life, you functioning in your world with all of your behaviors, responsibilities, joys, pains, pleasures, dislikes, and loves. The direction of Center asks you to be *in* the center and to *be* the center of your life and your universe. When you live from the center of your circle, you are grounded and centered—as awake, aware, and fully present in your self and in your life as possible, knowing what you are doing and why. This strong center provides a solid foundation from which to function in your life and to grow and expand. To be your own shaman, you must endeavor to know yourself and know how and why you function as you do in your life. With self-awareness, you can move more effectively from the center of your power circle to the horizon, the edges, the spirit worlds, and beyond. Center is you in the center of your power, in possession of your gifts and expressing them. It is the you that expresses your unique purpose in the world by drawing on the blueprint and the fuel found at the direction of within.

Center also has an intrinsic value beyond that which defines you personally and, as such, adds an element of balance, stillness, and gravity to your wheel. It is the core—the core of your life, your power, your self.

East: East is generally seen as the place of the rising sun and the rising moon, springtime, air, ether, wind, yellow, new beginnings, rebirth, new birth, infancy, renewal, planting seeds, abundance, prosperity, blooming, spirit connection, and gratitude.

South: South is typically the place of growth and healing, green, the midday sun and moon, summertime, transformational fire, red, puberty, passion, adolescence, maiden, warrior/hunter, creativity, entertainment, joy, flowering, music, personal connection with your inner child, power places where your soul song sings, and love.

West: West is often looked upon as the place of the setting sun and moon, autumn, orange, water, thunderstorms, rain, waterfalls, rivers, oceans, blue, divine union, midlife, parenting, teaching, harvesting the fruits of one's labor, collecting seeds, preparation for the end of a cycle, spiritual warrior challenges, clarity, spiritual questing, questioning, honoring mystical experiences, the ancestors, pondering, philosophizing, vision questing, and vision receiving.

North: North traditionally is the place of darkness, nighttime, twinkling stars, the aurora borealis, snow, ice, the cleansing of wintertime, rest, quiet, introspection, ancient knowledge, wisdom, the ancestors, the elements and foundation of the Earth, strength that comes from struggle, courage from challenge, wisdom gained from life's battles, enlightenment, the elder, the crone, the sage, and the journey of the death of the physical body and transition into the spirit world.

Above: Above is the place of radiant stars, the pulsating aurora borealis, cosmos, rainbows, clouds, weather spirits, thunder, lightning, Spirit of No Clouds, soaring winged ones, Grandmother Moon, Grandfather Sun, Father Sky, planet beings, the Upper World, and the great Void that is pregnant with potential.

Below: Below is the place of the beauty of all things natural, Mother Earth, nature spirits, faeries, gnomes, little people, small winged ones, animals, creeping and crawling ones, tree and plant spirits, the elements in combination, the Lower World, and the great Void at the center of the Earth that is pregnant with potential. These voids found in the directions *above* and *below* are similar and reflect the age-old benediction, "As above, so below. As within, so without."

Circle: Circle is the entirety of all of the energies and powers of the circle coalesced together. It is an energy force in and of itself, and is also the energetic container that holds all of the other energies and powers. The energy force of your circle has attributes that would be helpful for you to become familiar with. It may have a certain feel, vibration, color, texture, consistency, or movement. It may resonate with you in particular ways or in specific places in your body and energy field. When you connect with the direction of Circle, you will want to be aware of both the energy force of your circle and the energies contained by your circle. The powers of Circle are infinite, consisting of all that was, is, and has the potential to become. Circle unites all directions, things, energies, and powers, known and unknown, seen and unseen. In a very real sense, Circle is the grid that ties all the other points together. Just as the power spots of the Earth are connected by ley and dod lines, so too is your medicine wheel connected by the grid lines of circle. Circle is the rim, the surface, the interface, the boundary of your energy.

Within: Living from your center entails recognizing and honoring that which is within you, your soul-self and your core strength. Your soul-self is the essential essence of you, the life-force energy that is you. It is the light of the Creator within you and the spirit of you that lives in your body and will live on after this physical body dies. It is the energy source that makes up your luminous energy body and your authentic being. It is your primal, wild soul that is not domesticated by societal rules or fettered by your behaviors or the roles you play in life.

Within your soul-self there is an inner strength, a deep yearning, an internal impulse, and an intense fortitude that causes you to be alive and uniquely you. This core strength is both the fuel and the driver that strives to find expression in the world. It is the force behind your ability to manifest when you harness and direct your personal energy through focus, concentration, will, awareness, attention, and intention.

Within is also the way we connect to the Great Web of Life. We must seek the direction of Within in order to connect, through the soul in delta, to the totality of the universe. In a way, Within is the fuel of the wheel. While the other points define the structure, Within defines the fundamental source of power.

Journeys

Your circle of power is a circle that likely contains other circles within circles within circles. For example, it is common for shamans to have several circles that surround each other in all three worlds, making up the one large circle that helps them live their life, teach, and do healing work. Through your exploration, you may find that you have one or more circles of power in each of the three worlds that make up your power circle. With nine directions in three worlds and the possibility of several circles in each world, exploring these circles might seem time consuming and overwhelming at first. Please don't be discouraged. With just one journey you are on your way to connecting with the infinite powers of your circle. Anytime you can journey, it adds to your power base. Soon you will be quite familiar with your circle and enjoying the benefits of checking in often. It is recommended that you record your experiences in your journal and document the energies, powers, and attributes of your circle after each journey. Doing so will help you keep track of the many powers of the different directions. It might be helpful to draw a circle in your journal and write the powers around it in the directions where they appear in your personal wheel. Add to this living wheel whenever new additions come in. One of our students created a representation of her wheel on the computer by placing images, icons, and symbols of the powers within and around a large circle.

Journey Intention Suggestions

Your personal medicine wheel offers endless journey possibilities, so be creative. The following journeys can and should be repeated often for maximum benefit.

- Journey to the Upper World to the direction of Center. Experience yourself in the center of your life and the great wheel of life. Ask to be shown the medicines, energies, powers, and attributes in this direction. Allow yourself to receive any energies, powers, healings, teachings, and wisdom that are offered. Use all of your senses to experience this direction. Use your awareness to notice anything and everything about this direction. Repeat in the Lower and Middle Worlds.

- Journey to the Upper World to the direction of East. Follow the rest of the intention described in the Upper World journey to the direction of Center. Repeat in the Lower and Middle Worlds.

- Journey to the Upper World to the direction of South. Follow the rest of the intention described in the Upper World journey to the direction of Center. Repeat in the Lower and Middle Worlds.

- Journey to the Upper World to the direction of West. Follow the rest of the intention described in the Upper World journey to the direction of Center. Repeat in the Lower and Middle Worlds.

- Journey to the Upper World to the direction of North. Follow the rest of the intention described in the Upper World journey to the direction of Center. Repeat in the Lower and Middle Worlds.

- Journey to the Upper World to the direction of Above. Follow the rest of the intention described in the Upper World journey to the direction of Center. Repeat in the Lower and Middle Worlds.

- Journey to the Upper World to the direction of Below. Follow the rest of the intention described in the Upper World journey to the direction of Center. Repeat in the Lower and Middle Worlds.

- Journey to the Upper World to the direction of Circle. Experience all the energies integrating, circling, spiraling, connecting, and cycling. Follow the rest of the intention described in the Upper World journey to the direction of Center. Repeat in the Lower and Middle Worlds.

- Journey to the Upper World to the direction of Within and go deep inside yourself. Connect with your soul-self and your core strength. Follow the rest of the intention described in the Upper World journey to the direction of Center. Repeat in the Lower and Middle Worlds.

- Journey to the Upper World to the center of your personal medicine wheel. Experience yourself in the center of your life and the great wheel of life. Become as awake, aware, and fully present in and of yourself as possible. Notice what you experience. Ask to be shown a strength you have that you can use to empower yourself. Ask to be shown a weakness you have that you can strengthen to empower yourself. Ask your power circle to help you. Repeat in the Lower and Middle Worlds.

• Journey to any of the three worlds and meet with the energies, powers, and spirits of your power circle. Ask if it would
be beneficial for you to create a physical representation of
your circle in ordinary reality. If the answer is yes, ask for
guidance about how and what this representation could be
like. Remember, you are a cocreator in this process. Utilize
the information and images in exercise one (Creation of
Your Personal Medicine Wheel) and exercise three (Power
Circle Artwork).

Journey to your circle often. The more you connect with the power
in nonordinary reality, the more available and potent it will be in
ordinary reality.

Exercises: Connecting with Your Power Circle

Your power circle is with you all the time. To access it you need
to activate your awareness skills. The following exercises will help
you. They can be performed anywhere at anytime in ordinary consciousness or in nonordinary reality by journeying. Practice these
exercises as they are or, if you have the time and are in an appropriate place, enter into a journey for added relaxation and receptivity.
Either way, be sure to use your felt sense to fully perceive and receive the energies available to you through these exercises.

Begin each exercise by taking in a deep breath, closing your eyes,
and relaxing for a few moments. Relax and use the five-step process
of setting your intention, focusing, releasing, allowing, and accepting to help you become perceptive of and receptive to spirit connection. Ask your helping spirits to be with you and to help you connect
with them. Focus your attention and your intention on connecting
with your power circle.

Exercise One: Creation of Your Personal Medicine Wheel

Creating your personal medicine wheel in the physical world is a beautiful expression of your gratitude to your helping spirits and power circle and will help you readily access the energies of your circle and the Web. Take great care to make it sacred and special—a beautiful, powerful place to rest, rejuvenate, meditate, journey, perform ceremonies and healings, and to just *be*.

Your personal medicine wheel can be elaborate or simple—anything that you and your helping spirits decide. With spirit guidance, decide on the objects that you will place in your medicine wheel. A few examples are rocks, statues, pictures, stuffed animals, or special jewelry. Obviously, if you are creating an outdoor wheel, you will want to use weatherproof objects. Obtain the objects and then carefully choose a location, outdoors or in, to create your wheel. Ask permission from the energies and spirits there. If permission is granted, cleanse the space and the objects with the aid of the spirits and the cleansing methods of your preference.

Form a sacred circle with your intent and the help of the spirits. Rattle, drum, chant, sing, dance, and pray, asking all compassionate helping spirits and your power-circle energies, powers, and spirits to join you in sacred ceremony. A common way to call upon the power-circle energies is to acknowledge each energy and power in each of the nine directions. Begin in the center of the circle; relax and just observe. Notice the energy of the circle forming around you.

Connect with the Center by connecting with the center of the circle and yourself as the center of your life; connect with the direction of Within by connecting with your soul-self and inner core strength. Then one by one turn to face each of the four cardinal directions, Above, Below, Circle, and Within again. In each of the directions acknowledge and invite the energies and powers of that direction to join you. Focus and really see, sense, feel, and experience them with you. For example, one way to form a sacred circle after connecting with Center and Within is to turn to the East and say something like:

> I call to the compassionate helping spirits of the East and to my personal helping spirits who reside in the East, inviting each one by individual name. I call to the power of the place of the rising sun and the rising moon, of springtime, of the air and ether, and to the place of new beginnings and prosperity. I call to the energies and the powers of the East and invite you to join me in this sacred circle today. Please accept my deep, heartfelt gratitude for all of the light, power, energy, medicine, awareness, wisdom, guidance, healings, teachings, lessons, and love that you share with me and the world.

Then follow a similar pattern sunwise, or clockwise, around the circle. You will develop your own style and receive guidance from your helping spirits over the course of practice, so feel free to experiment and implement your own wording.

Once you have generated the energetic circle, put the objects in their designated places to form the physical circle. Take your time and do this mindfully and reverently. When you have finished, sit in the center of your circle and just be. Take in a deep breath and relax. Notice and observe how it looks and what it feels like. Meditate, journey, or do a ceremony to initiate and honor your circle. When you are finished be sure to thank the spirits and let them know that your work here today is finished.

Visiting and doing shamanic work in your circle often, as a part of your daily spiritual practice, will bring you great benefit.

Exercise Two: Power Circle

The Power Circle exercise helps you harness the power of your personal medicine wheel for anything, including energy, health, and wisdom.

Enter your personal medicine wheel and settle yourself in the direction of Center by settling in the center of the circle. Take in a deep breath and relax. Notice and observe yourself in your wheel. After a few moments, ask the helping spirits, energies, and powers of your power circle to come into ordinary reality as much as possible and form a circle around you. Use your felt sense to become aware and perceptive — see, feel, sense, and experience yourself inside of your circle of power. Notice how it feels to be surrounded by such power and protection, love and wisdom. Take your time and fully embrace this experience. Allow yourself to receive any energies, powers, healings, teachings, and wisdom that are offered. Use all of your senses to fully experience this exercise. Use your awareness to notice anything and everything. When it's time to return to your everyday activities, thank your power circle and say, "It is done for now."

As time allows, repeat this exercise at least eight more times and instead of staying in the Center, try experiencing what it's like to be a part of the circle in each of the eight other directions. In each direction notice and observe yourself in that direction, as well as observing the energies and powers of that direction. What are the wisdom, energy, learning, and medicine here? What can you learn about yourself from this direction? What energies and powers can you bring into use in your everyday life? Use your felt sense to experience and learn. Observe yourself, your energy body, and the circle.

After becoming familiar with the directions in individual exercises, you can vary this exercise by spending a few minutes in each of the nine directions during one exercise session. We also recommend exploring the in-between directions, such as east southeast, southeast, and south-southeast.

Exercise Three: Power Circle Artwork

Creating a personal medicine wheel in your back yard or in a room with objects, as you did in exercise one, is not the only way to create physical representations of your power circle. Sacred artwork such as drawings, paintings, mandalas, collages, jewelry, embroidery, weaving, knitting, and carvings depicting the patterns, symbols, and images of your power circle is a strong way to bring spirit energies and powers into your ordinary reality. Artistic talent is not a prerequisite for creating powerful artwork. Some of the most compelling art we have experienced might not win any prizes in the art world, but it definitely connects humans with spirit energies.

The key to doing this exercise is to get out of your own way and allow the experience to happen. Relax and use the five-step process of setting your intention, focusing, releasing, allowing, and accepting to open yourself to divine inspiration. Energetically cleanse yourself and your supplies with the cleansing methods of your choice. Invite your power circle to join you, and use your felt sense to experience it surrounding you. Center yourself in the circle; acknowledge the energies, powers, and spirits; and thank them with heartfelt gratitude. Begin your work. Cocreate in unison with them and allow their energies and powers to become the heart and soul of the piece. Craft whatever comes, without judgment. When you are finished (this may take more than one sitting), perform a small ceremony to initiate the piece and thank the spirits. Display and utilize your work reverently.

Exercise Four: Circle-Gazing Meditation

Power circle artwork can be used as a gateway into the Web. For example, in some cultures gazing into a mandala is a means of opening a portal into the universe. For this exercise you will be utilizing the sacred artwork of your power circle from exercise three.

This exercise can be done anywhere—in your personal medicine wheel, your soft space, or wherever you are. It is very simple yet can have profound results.

To begin, make yourself comfortable and use the five-step process to activate your perception and reception skills. Think of your intention and state it three times. You may want to explore and see what happens, or you can have a specific purpose, such as divination or healing. When you are settled and relaxed, stare into your power-circle artwork and allow yourself to journey into the image. Travel through the image and use your felt sense to experience anything and everything. Let go, and enter as deeply as you can. When you are ready to return to ordinary reality, travel back through your artwork and come back into your body. Be sure to thank Spirit.

As mentioned at the beginning of the chapter, we are part of many circles—community, church, alumni, social, professional. But the circles we value most are the circles that sustain us—our circle of friends, for instance, the people who listen to us no matter what we say and those precious few we can always count on. Family is another sustaining circle. The circle of our family is ideally the people who accept us as we are, warts and all. These are the people we can call in the middle of the night, if we need to, or can rely on to help us if we need it.

Unfortunately, even with wonderful family and friends, there are times when we feel truly alone. Life is full of those moments of indecision, weakness, or difficult crossroads when we need a strong hand or a clear eye to give us assistance or insight, but no one in our ordinary, physical-world circles is available.

At these moments our personal medicine wheel becomes more than just a practice or an exercise. At these moments the personal medicine wheel proves to be the circle that sustains us. By carefully cultivating our Spirit relationships in each of the directions, we quickly find that everywhere we turn, we have an ally. More than that, if we know the kind of help we need and we understand the spirit helpers we work with on our wheel, we will know just where to turn for tailor-made assistance.

In this work of self-discovery, fear is common—fear of the unknown, fear of change, fear of addressing our personal issues, fear of creating our own reality. Fear is always the first gate we must pass through in order to accomplish anything. Knowing that all of the friends of your personal medicine wheel are present with you at all times and are ready to help and defend you makes getting started a much more comfortable endeavor, even starting the most difficult or scary task.

How about if you need strength to lift something? Call on your friend the Earth from Below you. What if you need help with something new? All of your friends in the East would love to help. Too hot? Call in a North wind. Need to finish something? Call in the elements of the West. Need to find warmth and compassion in order to deal with a difficult situation or person? Flag down your pals in the South. Need some cosmic insight? Look Above. Need to understand why you do what you do? Your Center holds the key. Curious about your life's purpose? Your friends Within will help you.

Once we embrace our personal medicine wheel, we are never alone or without resource. We are sustained. We are safe. We are strong. It might be useful to think of your personal medicine wheel as your shamanic toolbox. It is what you will use, the tools of the trade you will employ, as you do your shamanic work. By the same token, it is your pitching bullpen. If you need counsel, help, expertise of any kind, your wheel defines the length and breadth of insight and power. The spirits that comprise your wheel are your power team, ever at the ready to pitch in when drawn upon.

Exploring and working with your circle is an ongoing process. Throughout your life you will change, and the energies and powers of your circle may change accordingly. Connecting regularly will keep you aware of any changes as well as connected to infinite energy. The extent to which your power circle is able to assist you in your everyday life is up to you. The more you connect, the more power and energy will be available to you. Practicing this chapter's journeys and exercises often will give you the vigor and inspiration to live your life fully.

CHAPTER SEVEN

Soul Healing

Who takes care of our spirit when it gets sick? We have doctors for the body, for the mind, and for the heart, but what do we do when our spirit is ailing?

— Sandra Ingerman, Soul Retrieval: Mending the Fragmented Self [ix]

At the moment she states the intention of her journey for the third time, the drumbeat carries her to her sacred, wooded departure point. Dancing around the campfire, she feels the power rising within her, and she soars low over the meadow, diving deep into the swamp. Careening through the tunnel, she enters the Lower World and meets Elk, her power animal. Hopping up on his back, she travels with him far across lush, green hills that seem to roll on forever. At the edge of velvety darkness, Horse and Owl join the journey. Passing easily through the veil, they enter a red-rock desert and encounter a warrior tightly bound to a crosslike structure, his hands tied to the horizontal branches and his feet barely touching the sharp rocks beneath. With no food, water, or relief from the heat, he wearily struggles for life.

She hops down from Elk's back and listens as her power animals communicate that he is symbolic of her spiritual warrior self, unconsciously left in the hot desert sun to suffer. She recognizes this warrior as a soul part of herself, vows to make changes in her life, and invites it to come back home. The pure energetic essence of the warrior is released from the self-imposed torture by her invitation and climbs aboard Elk's back. The warrior conveys that with the return of this energy she receives the gift of the ability to embrace, embody, and express her spiritual-warrior self. This gift will help her to be independent and strong in the face of adversity. With a deepened spirit connection, she will no longer feel that she has been left alone to suffer. Gratefully, she hugs her power animal and gathers in the pure, powerful energy of her warrior self, incorporating it into her very being. Elk, now riderless, looks at her and nods, honoring the fullness of newfound strength he sees in her.

As the shaman, the warrior essence within, and the three power animals travel on over green, rolling hills, a foreboding medieval castle appears shrouded in fog before them. The terrifying screams of a woman draw them inside. The cries lead them down to a dungeon, where they find her stretched out on a torture table, her limbs being torn from their sockets as the rack stretches and rips her spine. They are told that this gruesome sight symbolizes the fibromyalgia pain caused by power loss and the energetic/programmatic separation of body, mind, and soul. The soul part, represented by the tortured woman, begs for integration and shares that her return brings the ability to accept and embrace female power. Once freed from the table, the soul part stands in front of her, aligning chakra to chakra and energetically connecting to her via these bodily power points. The energies begin to run out of the soul part, moving into her like sand running from an hourglass, each chakra transferring itself to her, grain by grain. As the integration deepens and she accepts herself and honors her gender, her pain begins to dissolve. She suddenly realizes that she has believed that being a woman was limiting and oppressive and that her belief must change. By accepting and integrating this soul part, she is able to be whole. At the very moment she welcomes the change, the last grains of the soul part run out, projecting forward into her body and merging with her. Back in the soft space of the physical world, her body softly shakes with vibrant energy.

Leaving the castle and traveling on, they see several small soul parts floating like little energy bubbles on the light breeze. She is told she lost these soul parts through substance use. As she gathers them into a translucent, egg-shaped ball, they blend together and drift down to ride piggyback on her shoulders. In moments, she can feel them soaking into her heart and throat, warming, calming, and empowering her with their energy. These soul pieces collectively bring back the gift of being able to stay true to herself and to speak her truth with uncompromising honesty.

Moving on through a foreboding, dark forest, they approach a concealed cave. They cautiously enter and hear the soft cries of children keening through the darkness. Childlike energies reach out to them as they keep moving through the cave. It is very difficult for her to leave these energies, as she is trained and guided to do, so she wraps them in a warm blanket of love and healing energy, and prays to the spirits to help them find healing. Within moments, a faintly familiar voice softly speaks her name. She glances over her left shoulder just as a fleeting sparkle of energy congeals into the form of a small girl huddling in a corner. The girl appears to be about three years old, frightened, and alone. She can feel the intense fear throughout the girl's body, a message that helps her to consciously comprehend the unconscious fear that she deals with daily. Her small child-soul part shyly comes to her

and finally allows herself to be held. The tiny soul part telepathically tells her a story of loneliness. She believes that
no one loved her, held her, or told her she was wanted. She
cries uncontrollably. As she is comforted by the helping
spirits' intense love and spirit energy, the soul part's fear
dissolves, and the little girl hugs her so very tightly. They
remain in each other's embrace, eyes squeezed shut, tears
flowing. After a time, she opens her eyes and finds the girl
is gone, integrated back into her being, and she is clutching
herself in a hug of self-acceptance. She laughs out loud and
wipes her eyes, smiling up at Elk, who nuzzles her with its
warm, fuzzy nose. The return of the young girl's luminescent energy brings her the ability to accept and feel love.

They exit the forest cave, moving into a rolling meadow beneath a profoundly clear blue sky. Floating in the air above
them, like a balloon, is a soul part that was lost due to broken relationships. This soul part is airy and detached, making it easy to catch. She puts her mouth to the balloon and
breathes it into her. Ready to return, it easily blends with
the other parts. The returning soul energy brings her the
ability to connect with other people.

Throughout the journey, a magnificent Tiger has been joy-
fully pouncing in and out of her vision, orchestrating the
travel and assisting in the soul-energy return. This beautiful, regal Tiger communicates that it wants to join her and be
honored as her power animal. He tells her he has been with
her since birth and has protected her. Now he also wishes to
be a source of power and inspiration for her. As the sound
of the changing drumbeat signals her return, she gathers
in the energy of Elk and Tiger that have together created
a sphere of luminescent, vibrating energy. She reverently
holds the energy ball and then pulls it toward her, inviting

the energies to melt into her energy field and body. Returning to her departure point and back to her body, she slowly sits up and rattles around herself to seal in the energy.

If you want to make a real difference in your life and in the world, soul healing is the place to begin. It is the root of our work as shamans because our soul is the core of our being. In our healing practices and workshops we hear time and time again how amazing soul healing is and what a huge difference it makes in the lives of our clients and students. Folks often tell us how they have lived many years feeling empty or half dead, searching for healing, answers, and a passion for life. They have pursued years of therapy or practiced a variety of techniques, only to remain numb and dissatisfied. Then, in just one soul healing session or one journey, they connect with their soul, retrieve soul parts, and feel that they have experienced a miracle. How can this be?

To begin, let's consider this important question: do you *have* a soul, or *are* you a soul? We get all kinds of answers, but in the end shamans subscribe to the view that every person *is* a soul. Understanding this view is vitally important as we enter into the work of soul healing. Your soul is who you are—who you *really* are. Contrary to common thought, you are not who and what you think you are. You are not your thoughts, emotions, opinions, ideas, and what you do for a living. Those things are simply facets of where you came from and what you do. You are really something so much more. You are energy—pure, high-vibrational energy. If you have become disconnected from or lost some of this energy, then you are operating at less-than-full capacity and are likely dealing with myriad symptomatic issues of that energy loss. The simple, yet very powerful act of reconnecting with and retrieving this energy brings you back up to full capacity, giving you the energy to make a difference in your life and world. And your ability to make a difference is something we need now and in the coming times. The work that must be accomplished prior to being prepared to make a difference in the world is the work of integration in your own self. If you want to make a difference in the world, start with yourself.

In chapter one, we proposed the point of view that if the body is temporary and the soul eternal, then the soul must have a reason, an agenda, for occupying a human body. Shamans discern this agenda and use their bodies as instruments of communication between the soul/spirit realm and the world. Basically, the human body, mind, and emotions are tools that, when properly disciplined, can be utilized by the soul to make a difference for each person, their community, and the world at large.

But in order for the soul to express itself unhindered through us, we first need to understand exactly what it is, what it does, how the soul expresses itself, and what we can do to facilitate soul health and wellness.

Your Soul

Your soul is the pure spiritual essence that flows through, around, and within you. It is the source of your intelligence, your life, and defines your basic energetic nature. It is the life-force energy that sustains you. Your soul is layered, just as the mind and body are layered, and each successive layer resonates at a higher frequency. At the highest of these frequencies, your soul actually blends with and directly interacts with the universal energies of the Web of Life. Many disciplines around the world see these layers as separate bodies, labeling them as etheric, subtle, causal, and so forth. The higher the energy of the layer or body, the more difficult it is to access from this plane. But there are accounts, usually found in sacred texts, of individuals who have managed an awareness of some of these higher-vibrational levels of being. Because the powers and awareness these individuals are able to manifest are miraculous, we lesser humans often deify those who attain that level of mastery.

For our purposes, we will mostly focus on the human energy field produced by the soul and in the dynamics of the soul as it interacts with the closest of these higher universal energy layers. Indeed, we need exposure to the energies of the Web and its associated universal life force in order to stay healthy and alive on this denser physical plane. That said, we can see that the soul is comprised of both universal soul energy and individual soul energy. Your *collective soul* is the term we will use to describe the life-force energy you share with the greater whole—the oneness, macrocosm, Creator, Web, universe, Earth, other beings, and your human brothers and sisters.

Your individual soul, or soul-self, is the amalgam of all these energies as they flow within and around you. It is dynamic, not static, and is constantly commingling and interfacing with the creative energies of the universe itself and your personal energetic signature. Your soul-self is the multilayered, multivibrational, immortal essence of you. It is the light of the Creator within you and the spirit of you that lives in your body and will live on after this physical body dies. It is the energy source that makes up your luminous energy body and your authentic being. It is your connection point to spirit, the Web, and Great Spirit. It is the Godlike, Goddesslike, Christlike, Buddhalike spiritual divinity that is you at your most fundamental level. Being aware of this essential essence provides a sense of calm and strength. This soul-self is also the power source and the engine of creation you use from your center to create your personal reality through the manifestation of your beliefs.

Your soul-self is the originator of what we call extrasensory perception (ESP). It is your soul-self that gives you messages through your gut feelings, senses, intuition, inner knowing, and uncommon wisdom. It lies underneath your daily doings and the chatter of your mind. It is free from emotion and attachment to worldly aspirations. Your soul-self, without the chains of the world and the onus of our societal cognicentric conditioning, feels wild and free, and though it is childlike, is not childish. It is primal and authentic. It is dynamic and empowered. When you are aware of, connected with, and expressing this powerhouse within you, you create harmony and balance and sow the seeds of insight and awareness wherever you go and with whomever you speak.

Soul Expression

Your soul-self is you—within you and around you—but in journeys, ceremonies, and exercises it can sometimes appear separate from you. This is not because it is separate, but by giving the appearance of separation, it can communicate with you and be observed by you. It is sometimes difficult to see what is within ourselves, so this spiritual aspect of you may appear externally to be more tangible and observable. Your soul-self is also a part of the collective soul, so it is able to travel freely anywhere. This is why we say things like "my soul soars." Because of this travel ability, your soul-self may appear in different proximities to you in your journeys.

Your soul-self may also shape-shift, or change its appearance, to teach you about its nature, its attributes, and the gifts it brings to you for expression in your everyday world. It may appear as a separate energy or as a separate being. It may look like you or may take a form completely different from you in order to communicate its point or demonstrate something that may not be immediately obvious to you. It may be close to you or a ways away. Don't judge your experience. Where and how your soul-self appears in your journey-work does not indicate you're doing anything wrong or right. Its appearance and proximity are what it needs to show and teach you. Relax, release your expectations, and open your awareness to connect with this vital part of yourself, no matter where or how you experience it.

Your soul-self is intelligent and wise. It is your inner healer, your inner knowing, and your inner wisdom. Intuitive information, guidance, and healing energy will sometimes come externally from your helping spirits, and sometimes they will come internally, from your soul-self. These aspects of your soul-self are important for your health, well-being, personal growth, and spiritual evolution.

Your Soul Path

Your soul-self has an intention for being here on planet Earth in human form at this time. That intention is, in part, your personal spiritual evolution and the evolution of awareness. The particulars of each of these factors, in combination with your unique energy configuration, spiritual gifts, and specific function, determine your soul path. When your soul entered into a physical body in this world, it brought with it certain aspects. It brought life-force energy and essence, and it also brought learning, wisdom, insights, purpose, a mission statement or sacred contract, destiny, dreams, and needs that are designed to help it grow and evolve through experiences, expression, and awareness. Each of these aspects' level of importance in your personal spiritual evolution determines the idiosyncratic nature of your soul path. Your role in the evolution of consciousness may also determine your soul path.

The evolution of consciousness is a complex reality based on a simple concept. The life-force energy that creates and sustains us is intelligent and is seeking awareness of itself through our perceptions of it. The more aware we become, the more aware it becomes. As our souls become more spiritually evolved and aware, they shift the vibration in the consciousness of the Web, helping it become conscious and aware of its own intelligent energy. This shift has a ripple effect for all beings in the Web of Life and helps them become more evolved, aware, and conscious.

What this means to you is that in addition to your personal spiritual growth and evolution, you are here to assist in the evolution of consciousness. Your purpose, both personally and universally, determines your soul path, your spiritual work, and the experiences you will have in this life. It's not uncommon for clients to come to a shamanic session seeking knowledge about their soul path. They describe knowing they are here to do something very important and meaningful, but they just can't figure out what that is. This knowing or feeling of unrealized greatness is a common way that we experience the call of Spirit. They learn and practice spiritual- and personal-growth techniques that help them evolve, yet they remain "stuck" in traditional nine-to-five jobs that seem useless and mundane to them.

Many times, journeywork reveals that these people are meant to be in those jobs to help raise the consciousness of others around them and, ultimately, the consciousness of the Web. Not only are they there for their own growth, but they are also there to positively change the world. Simply by being an energy-filled light-being in the workplace, sharing their experiences and learnings with co-workers or even just demonstrating their awareness, creates powerful unconscious shifts. For many, understanding that they have this bigger assignment fills in the missing pieces of why they feel like they should be doing something important. They are doing or can do great things right where they are. Shamans don't live in caves in the mountains; they live in communities, where they perform mundane, everyday jobs alongside their sisters or neighbors. Shamanism is spirituality in the trenches. The way we interface in all situations and with family, friends, acquaintances, neighbors, and grocery-store cashiers has an impact. Making this a positive or substantive impact is a part of following our soul path. We have the ability to uplift the world with every interaction.

The extent to which you follow your soul path directly correlates with your ability to be impeccable. Following your soul path means right being and living for you personally. Impeccability requires that you be completely consistent within the parameters of your own beliefs—not your ego or your personality, but your authentic soul-self, which naturally expresses a divine connection and integrity.

For example, if your soul path is to evolve by teaching Reiki, and you are not doing this for any reason, you are not honoring your soul, soul-self, or soul path. It is your responsibility as your own shaman to know your soul path and to follow it to the best of your abilities. If you're not sure right now what your soul path is or whether or not you are following it, the journeys and exercises in this chapter will help.

Impeccability also depends on our soul being whole, energized, clear, and able to express itself through our resident programming and thinking machinery. Because a healthy soul is necessary for impeccability, it is also necessary to understand how souls get split, damaged, diverted, or starved for energy. This is the topic of soul health.

Soul Health

To be your own shaman, you must be responsible for recognizing and nurturing the needs of your soul. This entails honoring and connecting with your soul-self and honoring and following your soul path. When you take good care of your soul, the energy of your soul is readily available for health, happiness, well-being, living your life fully, and pursuing personal growth and spiritual evolution.

When your soul is not well cared for, the available soul energy available is compromised or blocked. Blocked soul energy can cause ailments that range from mildly irritating to debilitating. In shamanism, all ailments, illnesses, diseases, and failures to heal are energetic and spiritual in origin. Healing the soul heals the body, mind, emotions, and spirit.

Most people have some sort of spiritual ailment acquired through ignorance and neglect. We are not taught that nurturing our soul and honoring our soul path are as vital to health and well-being as getting a good night's sleep and driving carefully. Our technological, throwaway society has forgotten that the soul *is* our life, and that the level of harmony and balance you experience and the quality of your daily life correlate directly with the attention you pay to maintaining soul wholeness and wellness.

Soul-self disconnection is a consequence of soul neglect that causes various symptoms, ranging from negligible to severe, based on the extent of the disconnection. Symptoms such as fatigue, frequent or chronic illness, listlessness, depression, anxiety, fear, instability, powerlessness, addictions, loneliness, emptiness, spiritual voids, and spiritual hunger are common. Soul-self disconnection is similar to being disconnected from your helping spirits and your circle of power, except that the power you are disconnected from is that of your own soul and energy body.

Reconnecting with your soul-self directly links you with and opens up the flow of your personal life-force energy. Reconnection allows you to heal from health issues, satisfy your spiritual cravings, and rediscover the lost wild, free, primal part of yourself that reigned before the roles and rules of life robbed you of this power. Journeying to the wild soul inside of you, that *is* you, reconnects you with this powerful, dynamic energy, allowing you to harness strength, vitality, and reignite your passion for living. Journey to unleash your primal soul-self and experience being wild and free, dancing and soaring, and see if that doesn't help you heal and feel more alive!

Soul-path disconnection is far more common than soul-path connection. If we remember our soul's agenda as children, we soon forget it as we get caught up in the reality of our lives. The pressures of such things as societal conditioning, academic learning, fitting into society, being responsible, making a living, and raising children capture our attention, and we focus on the external aspects of making our lives happen. When we become separated from this important part of our own nature, we inadvertently lose connection with our soul's essence, goals, passions, dreams, and personal energy. Reclaiming our soul path reconnects us to our inner power and ultimately to energy and health.

There are also things that can happen to your soul that are beyond your control. Loss of soul energy and soul parts can occur from experiences the psyche views as traumatic. As your own shaman, you can heal your soul, bring back this lost energy, alleviate the effects of the wounding, and live dynamically.

Your soul is intelligent life-force energy that resides in and around your physical body. Everywhere you go and in everything you do you leave residual traces of soul energy. To the clairvoyant, we all look like we are emitting diffuse contrails as we go about our lives. If your soul is healthy and connected with the infinite energy of the Web, this normal phenomenon generally goes unnoticed. Soul loss or soul-self and soul-path disconnection can become problematic, as more and more energy is drained and not replenished. Even when we have a healthy soul, sometimes we unconsciously leave too much energy behind. When we have to separate from places and people that we love, it is normal to experience feelings of emptiness — "a hole in our heart" — and a longing to return. Usually this void dissipates over time. If it doesn't, we know that too much soul energy was lost, and we need to journey to reclaim it.

As we discussed, when we were tiny people, from our birth to about age three and a half, we downloaded a variety of beliefs about what is "real" in the world. We put all kinds of beliefs in place, like the nature of gravity, heat, cold — all that physical stuff. We also put in place beliefs about who we are and what really matters. We put in place the beliefs that guide us through our lives. Sometimes, though, a belief that is not necessarily helpful to us will get put in place. Maybe Mom leaves us in the car for too long on a hot day, and we instill a belief in ourselves that we don't matter. Maybe in that moment we see that if we want to be comfortable, we need to be in control. In that moment all kinds of inaccurate beliefs can be put in place.

The unfortunate thing is that as we get older, we write all kinds of programs to defend these beliefs. If the belief is that control is necessary for survival, then we accumulate all manner of behaviors that function to keep us in control. Over the course of our lives, we create a reality that reflects the beliefs we hold in delta, from when we were under four years old. Because we create this reality based on flawed beliefs and defend it with our programs, we will sooner or later run into trouble. The expression of the soul is being diverted by these programs and erroneous beliefs. Remember, the soul is the one that chose to be here, after all, and it wants to get busy doing what it came to do. It can't, though, because the programs are using up all the energy. Using our example, it's easy to see that it takes a lot of energy to be in control all the time. It's unnatural. Because it is unnatural, sooner or later this controlling individual will precipitate a problem that they cannot get out of without being hurt. In other words, our programs precipitate our own traumas in life.

But when trauma rears its ugly head, sometimes we just can't deal with it, so one of two things happens.

The first thing that can happen is called *soul loss*. This is when a piece of our soul goes away. It leaves because it either cannot or will not deal with the trauma. It can't deal with it, it cannot bear it, so it leaves. When it goes, it creates a hole in our soul and sometimes even in our memory. This hole must be repaired if we are to function as healthy, whole, effective shamans. In order to repair the hole, we must undergo *soul retrieval*.

The second thing that can happen is called *soul wounding* or *soul entrapment*. This happens when the trauma can be borne, but not processed. In other words, a bit of our soul pools around the memory of the traumatic event. When this happens, people will often say, "I just can't get over it," "I'm stuck with this," or "Every time I think of it, it all comes rushing back, and I'm there all over again." It is not soul loss per se, but it ties up such a great deal of our personal energy and soul attention that our expression of soul and our movement along our soul path is eliminated, or at the very least impaired. This situation is unacceptable for the soul if it is going to fulfill its agenda in the world. Many of the symptoms that appear after soul wounding are the soul pointing at the event, making sure our conscious mind is aware we have energy lost or caught in that event. There are a variety of methods for freeing the soul's attention and energy that is knotted up in soul wounding, and we will cover these in chapter nine. What follows is the methodology for attending to soul loss through self-soul retrieval.

Self-Soul Retrieval

When we have experiences that the psyche views as trauma, we unknowingly lose large parts of soul energy. Since the soul transcends time and space, it carries the living memories of all events and our response to those events, whether they are good times, success, celebration, hurts, trauma, or prolonged drama. Often a current emotional, mental, physical, or spiritual issue has its primary cause in residual trauma from a past event that caused soul loss.

Soul loss is a spiritual, emotional, and psychological illness that occurs when a part of the soul splits off. Soul loss is one of the most common and most detrimental spiritual illnesses, causing power loss as well as mental and physical debilitation.

It works like this: when we experience trauma, personal energy called a *soul part* leaves the person's body as a way of escaping the pain or discomfort. This departure is a normal, healthy coping mechanism that helps a person's psyche withstand the painful event. Soul loss may occur from experiences such as any type of abuse or neglect, abandonment, an accident, surgery, the breakup of a relationship, substance use, witnessing a traumatic event, the death of a loved one, or anything that causes emotional or physical pain. The trauma does not have to be considered severe to cause soul loss. It may also be induced through more subtle occurrences, such as separation from home on the first day of school or giving too much of yourself to your loved ones, family members, workplace, or clients.

If the soul loss is not rectified and the soul-part energy remains lost, this creates a void that prevents the person from being whole and functioning fully.

Soul loss can cause symptoms such as depression, anxiety, addictions, mental and emotional numbness, the inability to fully participate in life, a weakened immune system, frequent or chronic illness, and a feeling of emptiness inside. Modern psychology uses the term *dissociation* to describe this affliction and doesn't recognize the simple etiology of these devastating symptoms. Shamans know the cause and the solution—soul loss and soul retrieval.

You retrieve your lost soul energy and parts by entering into nonordinary reality using trance or journey techniques, connecting with your helping spirits and with their guidance, and traveling to the places where the soul energies and parts are. Your intention is to meet and retrieve any lost soul energies or parts that are ready, willing, and able to return. Your lost soul energy and parts may be found in any of the three worlds—sometimes waiting in the places they were left or lost, sometimes waiting in safe places in the spirit worlds. Your helping spirits will guide you to the places you need to go and help you retrieve the energy. Soul parts vary in appearance, as demonstrated by the journey story at the beginning of this chapter. It is important to release your expectations and follow the guidance of your helping spirits, since soul energy and parts go to different places for many different reasons.

Once the energy or part has been found, take a few moments to become reacquainted with it. The energy may have a message or a story to impart. It will also share the gift that is returning to you with its retrieval. The gift is often a personal attribute, such as self-worth, patience, or the ability to love fully, that was lost or compromised when the energy departed. Bringing back the soul energy brings forth the energy of the attribute. The gift may not always be something being returned, but something new that was never known. So again, release your expectations and allow your soul to communicate with you.

When your soul energy or part is ready to return and you are ready to receive it, ask it to return home by coming into you and joining the rest of your soul. Reach your arms and hands out into the air and gather in the energy lovingly and reverently. Bring your hands and the energy to your crown chakra, then to your heart, and then to your solar plexus. Breathe deeply and observe the energy soaking into your body and moving all the way to the core of your being. Notice the energy and how you feel. Take your time and remain quiet, relaxed, and open to your felt sense. After a few moments, ask if there are any more energies or parts that can return in this journey today. If there are, repeat this process. If you are finished for the day, thank your helping spirits and return to ordinary reality.

The most important gift of retrieving your lost soul energies and parts is the return of the energy of your soul. The information or the story that may have been shared is not the purpose of your retrieval. Your mind can use that information later to help you process and integrate the real healing: the return of your soul energy.

Relax and allow the energy to integrate within you for as long as you have time. We recommend planning your soul retrievals for times when you can take the whole day to care for yourself and fully experience the return of your soul power. Journal your experience, and then let it go. Try not to think about the retrieval for a while. Just feel the energy. Go for a walk, sit in the sun, listen to music — just be. Once you have allowed yourself ample time to integrate the energy into your body and soul, only then should you begin to integrate the experience with your mind.

It is not uncommon to have several or many lost soul energies or parts that are not able to come back in the same journey. To avoid energetic overload, ample integration time is often necessary before other energies or parts can return. Be patient, allow yourself plenty of time to integrate the energies already retrieved, and then periodically check in with your helping spirits to see if another soul retrieval is recommended.

Journeys

Journey in any of the three worlds, and meet with your helping spirits. As you do:

- Ask to see, feel, sense, and experience your soul.

- Ask to fly free as your soul. Explore the Web and the universe.

- Go Within and ask to meet your soul-self. If your soul-self is not in the Within direction of your personal medicine wheel right then, meet with it wherever it is.

- Ask to merge with your soul-self. Experience being wild and free, dancing and soaring.

- Ask to meet your soul at the time of incarnation. Carry on a conversation with your soul to learn about your soul path. Ask it such questions as: What is my soul path? Am I following my soul path? Have I wavered from my soul path? If so, how? When? Where? Why? Can I reconnect with my path now? Do the spirits or my soul-self have any guidance for me about following my path?

- Our soul speaks to us all the time. Are we listening? Ask your helping spirits to show you where, when, and how you can consciously perceive your soul's messages.

- Ask to be shown when, where, and how your soul-self communicates with the ego or consciousness self.

One of the ways that we can function more harmoniously is to let our soul, not our ego, run the show. When we go about our daily lives, we are often operating from our programs and conditionings in our consciousness or ego center. As we work on dismantling, deleting, and rewriting these programs, we can also learn how to live more in sync with our soul by living from our soul center that exists in delta—the "authentic self" without masks, identities, programs, or projections.

- Ask what living from your soul center means to and for you. Don't do anything; simply observe and learn.

- Return to the previous journey and ask to be shown when you can live from your soul center. Spend the entire journey exploring all the different situations and places where you can live from your soul center. Also explore the people who will support you living from your soul center.

- Return to the previous journey and ask to be shown how to live from your soul center. How do you let your soul run the show? How do you get your programs to step aside? How can your soul manage to express itself around, over, or through the programs? How do you remain awake and aware and acting, doing and thinking, from the soul?

Do an exploratory journey to see if you have any lost soul energies or parts. If you do, ask if you are ready to perform a self-soul retrieval. If the answer is yes, perform the soul retrieval as described with the guidance of your helping spirits.

When journeying or preparing to journey for self-soul retrieval:

- Ask your helping spirits to assist you.

- Ask to meet with the helping spirits that will be working with you during self-soul retrievals. Find out who they are, how they work, and as much information about self-soul retrieval as you can.

- Ask your helping spirits to help you reclaim any lost soul energy that you know you left in a specific place, situation, or with a certain person.

- Meet with the soul energies or parts that just returned. Welcome them home and inquire about their needs. Learn what you can do to integrate and honor this precious soul energy.

- Ask to reclaim any lost soul energy that you know you left in a specific place or situation or with a certain person.

Exercises: Engaging Your Soul-Self

Exercise One: Meet and Merge with Your Soul-Self

You can connect with your soul-self anytime and anywhere simply by becoming aware. Connecting with your soul-self is incredibly energizing and enlightening, and you were meant to function with this full connection in place all the time.

Begin by taking in a deep breath. Exhale and relax. Relax your shoulders and your neck. Close your eyes. Release your everyday thoughts and doings. Take in another deep breath, exhale, and relax. Feel your mind quiet and your whole self become calm and peaceful. Focus your attention and your intention on connecting with your soul-self.

When you feel relaxed, invite your soul-self to appear. Be open and receptive to who or whatever appears. Use all of your senses to experience the energy of your soul-self. You may not be able to "see" it, so notice what you are feeling, experiencing, and sensing with all of your senses. When you have connected with your soul-self, ask for some words of inner guidance, wisdom, or a healing, if it feels appropriate. Open your mind and soul, and receive this gift with your heart.

Your soul-self emits energy that is your soul energy and that should therefore resonate strongly with your own energy body. Feel the high-vibrational energy that comprises them both. Notice how your energy feels being in the presence of this soul energy. Can you see, sense, or feel your own brilliant energy glowing before you? Check in with yourself. Do you notice your energy body "light up" as you experience the high vibration that emanates from this powerful soul energy? See, sense, feel, and experience all the ways that your energy body changes by being in the presence of your soul-self. Ask your soul-self to let you fully see, feel, sense, and experience its energy clearly so that you can recognize the energy, aspects, nuances, patterns, vibrations, sound, color, and form it takes, if any. Ask it to tell you about its and your energetic qualities and attributes. Listen with your heart. Don't worry if it feels silly. Remain open and accepting of whatever comes to you.

If your soul-self appears separate from you, invite it to merge with you. Ask it to step inside your energy field so that you can become one again. See, sense, and feel it standing and directing in front of you, lined up chakra to chakra. When you feel yourselves fully lined up, allow the merging to take place. Open up your energy boundary using your intention, and feel your soul-self step into your energy field. See, sense, feel, and experience your energies blending. Experience yourself filling with dynamic high frequency energy. Sense, see, feel, experience, and receive for as long as you have time. Sit quietly and feel the power.

When you are finished with the exercise, thank your soul-self for this experience. Your soul-self is you, so there is no need to disengage. Maintain the connection and the energy flow as you go about your everyday activities.

We recommend practicing this exercise often to keep your connection with your soul-self strong and healthy. If it was difficult for you to connect with your soul-self, it is especially important that you repeat this exercise regularly until your connection is firmly reestablished.

Exercise Two: Expressing the Soul

There is a certain feeling that we all have when we are "in the flow" and expressing our soul. To begin, notice what you are thinking. After a few moments, take in a deep breath and send your conscious awareness down deep into your guts. Relax your thoughts and become aware of your feelings. Notice things like whether you feel sad or happy, grumpy or tired.

Now take in another deep breath, slow your mind down even more, relax deeply, and become aware of your emotions. Pay attention to the deep rumblings inside of yourself, noticing things like a sense of strength and well-being or of fear and unrest.

Now take in another deep breath and slow down even more. Stop thinking, and just sit quietly. In the cracks between thoughts and feelings we can sense our own soul flowing through us. When we communicate to others from this soul center, we express the soul and say wise things that surprise even us as they come out of our mouths. Notice how it feels to experience the world from this feeling, sensation, and orientation. The more you practice sensing your soul's expression, the more familiar you will become with this feeling and the more comfortable you will be living your life from this center of awareness.

CHAPTER EIGHT

The Luminous Energy Body

It is better to light one candle than curse the darkness.

—Chinese proverb

Lying on her magic blanket, she repeats the intention of her journey three times and allows the rhythmic drumbeat to carry her to her sacred wooded departure point. Building personal power by dancing around the campfire, she shape-shifts into the form of an owl. Feathers and wings replace skin and arms as her appearance and consciousness alters. Soaring over the treetops and angling toward the swamp, she dives into the cool water, careening down the tunnel into the Lower World, where she meets her power animals. They immediately guide her to perform an extraction on herself.

With eyes closed in a trance-state, the shaman sits up and rattles around her body. Setting aside the rattle, she scans just above her body, and her hands seek sensory messages. She is first drawn to her heart center, where she feels excessive heat and the thick, sticky energy of emotional injury. Levitating her hands just above her heart, she sees dark protrusions of spiritual energy that appear like darts piercing her aorta. As she retains this vision, several crows sweep in and pluck away the black barbs, leaving emptiness in their wake. She holds the energetic space as they perform their healing duties. Finishing their work, the crows scatter as quickly as they appeared. Removing the intrusions has left a void, which she carefully fills with the energy vibrations of love and with swirling rainbow colors.

Sensing that her heart is full, she further scans her energy field, stopping at her abdomen when she feels a large pocket of excessive heat. In a flurry of activity, her helping spirits rally around her and begin to extract a long, ropelike cord from her uterus. The sticky, black, sinewy cord seems endless as they pull and pull. Every foot or so of cord they remove she rolls into an energy ball and places into a bowl of transmuting water. As she rolls, hand over hand, the twining energy gradually releases its hold on her body, thinning and lightening as the end nears. At last the cord releases from the core, and the heat subsides, leaving behind a scattered mist of emotional residue. Gathering this smoky gray substance into a ball, she places it in the water to transmute it. A long-held belief, one that tells her that she is unwanted because she is female, begins to evaporate as her tears express the release she feels in her body. The resulting vacated space is filled with healing spirit love and life-force energy that are conducted through the hands, paws, and hooves of her helping spirits. Swirling rainbow energy reverberates through her body, holding her in a state of grace that balances and revitalizes her essence.

Detecting the change in drumbeat, she retraces her path up the tunnel through the swamp to the campfire of her departure point. As the final beats pulsate, she draws her essence back into her soft space and into her body.

In chapter one, we mentioned that shamanism is a discipline that requires awareness and the application of that awareness with responsibility. Up to this point in the book, we have worked on cultivating
awareness and applying it to ourselves. We now begin to refine our
own techniques for awareness and extend them out into the world.
We don't have time to waste—none at all, in fact. We have to collaborate on the movement that will turn the tide in this reality. This
is where the "application with responsibility" comes in. We have
done the work to observe what is. Now we need to facilitate the
birth of what can be.

The body's natural state is vibrant health. The mind's natural
state is free-flowing, receptive awareness. The soul's natural state is
one of open expression, empathy, intuition, insight, and substantive
action that makes a difference in the world. We can see, however,
that this ideal is rarely fully realized in us personally and certainly
not in the human race as a whole.

If we are naturally meant to be healthy, happy, mentally alert,
and engaged with the world, then why does it seem like everyone
has so many unresolved issues? Why are there illness and disease,
depression and anxiety? Why is it so hard to get up in the morning
and be a shining beacon of light in what seems to be an increasingly
darkening world?

To a certain extent, we can hang these issues on the way our
thinking machinery was originally programmed. Hindu scholars
say we are currently at the lowest point of the Kali Yuga, or Age
of Iron, of the 24,000-year grand cycle of Yugas described by the
Vedic Doctrine of World Ages. This Kali Yuga, a 2,400-year cycle
in itself, is characterized by gross materialism, ignorance, conflict,
confusion, arrogance, spiritual darkness, and everything running
contrary to our divine potential. We have thousands of years of generational programming that reflect a descent into this darkness. The
programming we were loaded with—our beliefs, behaviors, and social mores—were to a certain extent corrupt at the outset. As any
computer programmer will tell you, manifested results are only as

good as the software that's running. Or, more quaintly put, "Garbage in—garbage out." In essence, we are troubled, sick in body and mind, and suffering because we are a product of this age of man. Not a very uplifting sentiment.

The good news is that we are at the nadir of the descent. It is unlikely to get significantly worse. Not to say we aren't in for some rough road ahead—we are. It's still dark in here, and the darkness requires its due. But overall, the coming age will be characterized by a slow but steady improvement of our circumstances, with an increase in energy and a higher vibration in the Web that we will be able to perceive and potentially utilize. This shift will be facilitated by the applied focus and intent of those who are willing to do the necessary personal and spiritual work. If you are reading this book, you are one of those who will be making this transition happen. You will participate in it by cultivating awareness, repairing and revitalizing your own energy body, and tapping into the deep, abiding, and sustaining energy of the Great Web of Life. By increasing your own vibrational level and teaching others how to do the same, you will be participating in the beginning of the groundswell that will move us past this low point and start us on our ascent toward another golden age of humankind.

That might sound like an awfully big bite to take, but the early steps of this shift begin with the decision to learn about, repair, and maintain our own luminous energy bodies. To do that, we need to start with the basics. We first need to learn the architecture, nature, and fundamental dynamic of the human luminous energy body. We then need to understand the challenges this energy body faces; how to meet and move through those challenges to vibrant health and clarity; and then how to facilitate that same repair in our communities and the world. In a way, what we are doing is repairing the damage to ourselves, rewriting the programming, and then helping our communities repair and rewrite theirs. In so doing, we move out of this darkness and position ourselves to move into the light of the coming age.

To accomplish this, we need to begin where all good inquiry begins.

Part One: Personal Energy and the Human Luminous Energy Body

To those who can see the human energy body, it looks like a large, luminous egg that surrounds and infuses the physical body. Its outermost boundary layer averages roughly one arm's-length distance from the physical body and surrounds it completely. Shamanic wisdom states that the luminous egg, or energy body, is an emanation of the soul itself and is bolted to the body by a series of energy vortices. The layout of these "bolts" varies according to culture, but for our purposes, it is useful to view the bolts corresponding in vibration, color, and location to the seven classic chakras. These are the root or earth chakra (red), found at the base of the spine, at the point where the legs meet the lower body; the sex or sacral chakra (orange), located in the genitals; the power or solar plexus chakra (yellow/gold), sitting between the navel and the solar plexus; the heart chakra (green), found in the center of the chest; the throat chakra (blue), located in and around the larynx; the brow, intuitive, or third eye chakra (indigo), positioned between the eyebrows; and the crown or mystic chakra (violet), sitting at the top of the head. These seven chakras emit chakra-specific vibrations that flow throughout the human energy field, combining to create the color and luminescence characteristic of the individual's energy body. (As an aside, shamans in certain cultures, especially those in parts of South America, "unscrew" these chakra bolts, allowing the soul to separate from the body so that they can examine and work with the soul more easily. Separating the soul also gives the body a brief respite from a damaged energy body as the latter is being worked on and healed.)

The luminescence of the energy body is seen shamanically to be evidence of spiritual health and an unhindered flow of energy, flowing out through the body and energy field as an expression of the soul. The energy body is contained by a boundary that is also made up of seven parts, layered one on top of the other, like the layers of an onion. Each layer of the boundary corresponds in vibration and location to the chakras; the innermost layer reflects the root chakra's red color and vibration, and the outermost layer reflects those characteristics of the violet crown chakra. To an observer, the overall color of the luminous egg, also known as the aura, is determined by the dominance of a particular layer or chakra, which may reflect the individual's level of development and vibration. Aura color also indicates the overall health of the individual and the energetic state they may be experiencing at the time.

As mentioned, the energy body is fueled from the same source that all of our personal energy originates from—our soul—and for all intents and purposes is a closed system. The energy body of a typical person interfaces with the greater source of life-force energy inherent in the Web only during moments of deep, dreamless, delta-wave sleep. Even then, it is the soul that makes the contact, drawing in the needed universal life-force energy to sustain and revitalize us. For most of us, this energy gathering is as conscious an act as hormonal regulation or blood-electrolyte balance. It happens unconsciously and automatically in the vast majority of people. For shamans, dipping into this sea of life-force energy is an act of choice and practice. By doing so, shamans maintain and repair their own and their client's energy bodies through conscious intent.

This energy-body healing wouldn't be necessary if we never had to face any energetic challenges. But facing challenges is what life is all about. Unfortunately, these challenges can damage our energy body. Trauma can cause rips and tears in its boundary layers, and unwise attachments or addictions can link us to people, situations, or substances that drain us. More than that, there are all manner of opportunistic influences that can prey on us. Because all of the afore-mentioned challenges (trauma, opportunistic influences) can damage our energy body, a shaman has to know what to look out for.

We might understand the energy body and the human energy dynamic, but before we can learn how to repair it and maintain it, we need to have a feel for what can go wrong.

Energy and Health Challenges

There are as many challenges and ills that can assault the energy body as there are diseases and maladies that can infect or debilitate the mind, emotions, and physical body. As we have discussed, all illness begins in the layers of the energy body, and from there it de-scends into the physical, mental, and emotional. Therefore, problems in the emotions, mind, and physical body directly reflect a problem in the energy body.

For instance, not too long ago, a gentleman came for shamanic treatment on the great pain he was experiencing in his hips. He was trying to avoid surgery at all costs. He was also exhibiting chronic bad breath, which was the result of his teeth literally rotting in his mouth, and he exhibited fierce and deeply held racism. He had been everywhere to try to eliminate the pain in his hips, spending thou-sands on massages, Reiki, painkillers, and chiropractic treatments, but had only managed temporary relief. From a shamanic stand-point it was obvious that none of these treatments would provide a lasting cure, because none of them were addressing the energetic cause. Every one of the well-intentioned practitioners had treated his hips, given him a breath mint, ignored his racism, and sent him on his way. It took only a relatively short interview to verify that the man's racism was founded in an early life event and belief sys-tem put in place by his father. He was energetically blocked and stagnant in his root chakra because of the way he was orienting himself to the world through his racist stance. His bad breath and rotting teeth were the by-products of spewing forth the negative, prejudicial hate-mongering he was known for. The energy had quite literally gone bad in his throat chakra. It was necessary to help him rewrite that racist belief by unloading the events surrounding the original downloaded programming from his father, extract the negative and foul energies, and teach him how to get the energy flowing freely again throughout his energy body. Once all of that was done, his hip problems straightened right out. He now leads a happy and healthy life. Unfortunately, his teeth were too far gone and had to be removed. He chose to see their removal as a purging of old, outdated ways and an end to the generational karma his family had long perpetuated, so he was not traumatized further. Rather, he was empowered by this alternate point of view—and a brand-new set of dentures.

This is just one example of how physical and emotional illness, disease, pain, and discomfort come from spiritual and energetic imbalances that begin their existence in the energy body. What causes imbalance? Anything and everything can be a cause, based on a person's individual experiences, perception, beliefs, and points of view. Trauma of one form or another is a classic unbalancer. Car crashes, accidents on the job, beatings or abuse, breakups and divorces, loss of a loved one, stress, addictions and other habits, ingrained behaviors, strongly held disadvantageous opinions, negativity of all kinds, illness, pain or discomfort, near-death experiences, lying or falseness, subterfuge or wearing a "mask," an inability to adapt to change, or anything that clashes with deeply held beliefs could be seen as unnatural, or as a trauma, and therefore may yield an imbalance.

Influences from exterior forces may also play a factor in creating an imbalance in a person's energy body. Intrusions, attachments, curses, psychic attacks, exposure to psychic or energy vampires, possession, manipulation by skilled sorcerers, and unintentional energy linkages to those who drain us are a few examples of these forces. It is important to approach these kinds of assaults from our exterior very circumspectly. It is not necessary to get in an energetic battle with someone who has cursed or attacked you. Their actions have their own price that that person must pay. Your job as personal shamanic practitioner is to direct your attention to your energy and remedy the imbalance rather than engaging in pointless conflict. That which we give energy to, we give life to. It is never to your best advantage to energize an attacker. The best defense is to be impervious. Being impervious is also the reward you receive from doing the energy work and from paying attention to where your energy is being spent and to how fluidly it is moving through your energy field. We recommend that you release and transmute negative energies that make their way to you. You might address or acknowledge the source, but you should never retaliate. Once you do, you have picked an agreement to give a particular disadvantageous reality substance and importance. This reality will never serve you. It's the trap of self-indulgence the attacker looks for and should be avoided.

The ways that these myriad stimuli result in imbalance varies. Some extreme traumas can rip or tear our energetic boundary layers, allowing energy to leak out. In other instances, energy cords link us to others and continue to drain us until they are severed. Sometimes energy gets locked in a situation, and we cannot extract it. In many instances, we stand in our own way by being at odds with ourselves.

All of these imbalances show up in the energy body, and all of them require one of a variety of energy-oriented solutions. Each of these solutions activate and strengthen a person's energy flow, energy field, and energy boundaries.

Healing and Cleansing the Energy Field and Body

While the causes of illness or imbalance are unique and nuanced, they generally fall into a few broad categories. Each of the following energetic problems has associated traditional shamanic approaches for healing them. These can be found in a handy chart in the appendix located at the back of this book.

Counteracting Lethargy and Energy Stagnation: This is one of the most common problems we see in shamanic practice. It is also one of the earliest warnings that illness may be on the way, if left unattended. Fortunately, it is the easiest to fix. Many times we subvert energy that should be "in the flow." Circumstances demand that we adopt behaviors that are unnatural or that cause us internal conflict. Stress at work is a prime example of this type of circumstance. Demands and obligations that force us to deny ourselves or our family cause a pooling of energy. Resentment might initially cause this pooling, or perhaps concern over the issues of daily living. In any case, the pooled energy must be restimulated to move back into the flow. This is done by one of a variety of energy-movement exercises. We recommend chakra spinning, which is performed by closing your eyes and visualizing each of your chakras spinning clockwise, glowing vibrantly with their appropriate color. You can also then visualize the energy flowing out of each chakra, down the left side of the body, back up the right side, down the front of the body, and up the back. Then picture the energy gathering at the feet and fountaining up through the body along the spine and out the top of the head. From there it cascades down and coats the interior of the luminous egg, misting through the entire energy field and clearing away and dissolving any disadvantageous energy.

Energy Blockages: Sometimes the pooling of energy over a prolonged period of time can result in an energy blockage: energy that has solidified into an obstruction that keeps any other energy from flowing past or around it. Blockages are the last energetic step before illness manifests in the emotions, mind, and physical body, and can be caused by all manner of things. Cognocentricity (thinking one is right all the time), habits, addiction, stubbornness, negativity, stored emotions, and abuse or physical trauma are all forms blockages can take. One way you can tell if you have an energy blockage is to listen to yourself describe your perception of your problem.

You might catch yourself saying things like "I just can't get past it" or "I'm stuck" or even "I feel blocked."

There are three ways we treat this phenomenon. One is extraction, the equivalent of energy surgery where the obstruction is actually removed. Extraction and dismemberment, the second method, will be covered in the next section on intrusions. The third method is to energetically dissolve the blockage using the focused energy combined with visualization. Close your eyes and focus on the blockage, where the energy is caught. See the blockage in whatever form it presents itself to you. If you can, have a dialog with it and ask it how to dissolve or remove it. If you get an answer, try that. If not, try visualizing little Pac-men eating up the blockage, a stick of dynamite blowing it up, a snake consuming it, or an energy drill pulverizing it. Then focus the energy of your energy body so that it flows over and around the remnants, dissolving them all until there is nothing left.

Intrusions: Sometimes, things can get lodged in our energy body. An unkind word, a trauma, an injustice, or just old issues can "stick in our craw." Other times, attachments by benign energy entities, darts flung at us from psychic attack, or any number of different kinds of undesirable energies, called intrusions, can end up lodged in us. When this happens, the shaman employs a method known as extraction, which was demonstrated in the story at the beginning of this chapter. Extraction is performed during a journey and with assistance from one's helping spirits. It involves locating the source of the problem—the intrusion—and energetically removing it.

The personal shaman begins by journeying to a healing place in the Otherworld and connecting with the helping spirits that help perform extraction. The shaman then scans their energy field and physical body, looking for any intrusions or blockages. Once they find the intrusion, the shaman will speak with it, ask it to tell its story, and then encapsulate it in energy, scoop it out, and remove it from the body. Often, the shaman will place the intrusion in a crystal, a bowl of water, or a pile of sand. These natural substances dissipate the energy over time, taking it out of the world and transmuting it into energy that nature can recycle.

Dismemberment, used as an initiation in many shamanic traditions, is another powerful way to remove intrusions as well as energy blockages. Dismemberment entails journeying to a medicine place in the Otherworld and asking the helping spirits to facilitate a shamanic death for the purpose of healing. In the journey, the journeyer will typically experience a metaphoric physical dismemberment and death that are extraordinary, while their actual physical body, present in the soft space, experiences no pain or discomfort. Once bodiless, the shaman will experience what it is like to be spirit energy, free of the confines of the physical. Prior to the callback, the body is reassembled, or "re-membered," minus debilitating intrusions and blockages. In addition to the energy cleansing that takes place, this journey usually results in the shaman feeling reconnected to the soul-self and the divine in new ways. The dismemberment/death also releases the stronghold of the ego as we know it to facilitate the birth of a new self that is reconnected to the Web of Life. The concept of this journey may seem a little strange or frightening, but we assure you, it is safe and remarkably beneficial. Trust yourself and the relationship, guidance, and teachings of your helping spirits.

Energetic Attachments Infrequently, intrusions are found to be caused by intelligent inorganic entities, spirits of the uncrossed dead, or their energetic influences. Folklore is filled with stories of individuals possessed by "demons," and the horror movie genre is full of such images. But in actuality, these demons, which we call inorganics, are just tenacious entities that like living in a body. We humans are unique. We taste, touch, eat, and drink. Our senses are a playground for us. Sometimes spirits or inorganics want to come play on our playground, and when an individual is run down or traumatized, these entities can enter the human energy body and attach themselves to it. When this happens, the person may feel "not themselves," and their friends may report that the person "had a complete personality change." These descriptions are tip-offs that the person may be possessed by either an inorganic or an uncrossed spirit.

In both cases, the personal shaman approaches the entity attachment as they would an extraction. When confronted, the shaman may have a more intense exchange with the entity than they would with a self-induced blockage or energy intrusion, but the end result is the same. The shaman has the advantage of being alive and a citizen of the physical world. Energy entities that prey on the weak are neither. Inorganics can be lured, beguiled, driven off, commanded to leave, or banished. With an uncrossed spirit, the shaman can provide counseling and an escort service to the Otherworld.

Spirits of the dead can get stuck in this plane for a variety of different reasons. It may be that they are afraid to cross over, are confused about how to cross, have a story to tell, have unfinished business, have a message to impart to the living, or just want to stay because they enjoyed living so much. In rare cases, these spirits will attach themselves to the living. When a shaman finds a spirit attached to themselves, they must extract it and encourage it to crossover using a method called psychopomp. Usually, all the shaman needs to do is to listen to the uncrossed spirit's story and encourage the spirit to move into the light, which will automatically allow it to move on to the next world. Sometimes, though, the spirit does not want to leave or know how to go. In these cases, the shaman can call in to the next world to bring the spirit's loved ones to this side of the light in order to help the uncrossed spirit move on. This nearly always works, but in the extremely rare case that the spirit will not cross, we suggest seeking the assistance of a reputable shamanic practitioner.

Energy Boundary Leakages: Another common energy problem is the loss of energy through a ripped, punctured, or split energy boundary. When a person experiences trauma involving intrusions, possession, or attachments, the energy boundary is often left with a hole in it. That hole or tear bleeds personal life-force energy indiscriminately out into the ether, just like a puncture in a plastic bag allows water to seep out. Because leakages are associated with intrusions or trauma, sealing them is usually the second step in the extraction process. Still, sealing an energy leak stands alone as a process in itself.

When a personal shaman finds a leak of this nature in themselves, they journey to the spot on the energy body where the leakage is occurring. Again, a discussion with the tear, rip, or hole is encouraged. This discussion will reveal whether the cause of the leak is an ongoing problem, habit, or circumstance that can be addressed in physicality so that it does not continue to reinjure the energy body. Once the shaman understands the story of the leak, they seal it up with energy. Some visualize it healing just like a cut would heal — the sides rising to cover the injury and leaving the energy boundary leak and scar free. Some practitioners knit together the opening as a surgeon can sew together a wound, stitching the sides together so that the natural processes of the energy body will finish the healing process. One shaman of our acquaintance sees a rainbow vortex that swirls from the inside of herself out to the leak, vibrating the aperture to heal while eliminating the leakage of energy. Any of these techniques work equally well. Choose the one that works best for you, or journey to your helping spirits and ask them the best method for sealing such an energy wound.

Cords and Energy Links: Another common problem that people experience is energy draining through links or cords that connect individuals with another person. These links or cords are unlike many energy-body problems in that they are generally taken on voluntarily by the person suffering the problem. Anytime one person takes responsibility for another, an energy link or cord is created. Obviously, the most common form of this phenomenon is the parent-to-child link. Another is the spousal link. Unfortunately, cords and links are also formed when people try to do good deeds and take away the responsibility of another through compassion or generosity. This sounds harsh, but too much of a good thing is damaging. We cannot and should not try to take responsibility for another. In so doing, we steal away their life lessons, their opportunities to grow, and their chance at securing their own freedom. That is not to say empathy should not be employed in everyday life. Of course it should. But the natural extension of responsible empathy is a hand up, not a usurping of personal sovereignty. For instance, it is very common for practitioners of a variety of healing modalities to link with the energy of their client in order to facilitate healing. If that link is not severed at the end of the session, that same practitioner's energy can be drained by the very client they were trying to help. It's not the client's fault. It's just that the link was sustained past the point of usefulness for both client and practitioner.

If you find energy cords draining you, we recommend that you first visualize your energy body in its totality. Then investigate the cords and links, looking into the whys and wherefores for each one's existence. Once that is done, envision a knife, sword, or any cutting tool of your choice cutting the cords and links away. See the linkages falling completely away and the spot of attachment healing up completely. Then examine and determine why the situation presented itself in the first place, so that you can take action to prevent it from happening again.

Inability to Receive Energy: It is an unfortunate common occurrence in our culture that folks often cannot or will not receive energy to replenish the energy they may have lost or that is being drained from them. This inability to receive energy may stem from feelings of inadequacy, the belief that they do not deserve to receive, the belief that they are unworthy in some way, or perhaps just a lack of knowledge about how to receive. If you find you cannot receive energy, we encourage you to see that you are part of a greater whole and that in order to advance you need to learn how to nurture yourself. Part of that process is to open to the energies of the universe. Journey to your helping spirits and ask for help with opening to universal life-force energy and seeing it entering into you, sustaining you, and nurturing you. Perhaps it would be helpful for you to see yourself immersed in a cosmic bath of energy that warms and sustains you.

You deserve it, and it feels good. So go ahead, let the life-force energy flow into you, through you, and back out into the world.

Part Two: Universal Life-Force Energy

So far we have discussed the nature of the energy body and the ways to maintain and repair it, but without understanding the nature of energy in the universe, we are not doing quite enough to benefit ourselves, communities, and the world. Right here is the litmus test for a true shaman. Shamanism is not a solely contemplative practice. Shamans employ an engaged mysticism that includes service. If a person is willing to contribute to the greater good, get in the trenches and make a difference, then they are a shaman.

In order to affect the greater good, we must understand the bigger picture. The truth is that we are not an island. We are not bubbles of consciousness floating about the world, working towards our own gratifying enhanced self-awareness. Rather, we are spikes of self-awareness rising out of, but still connected to, a sea of oneness, using that isolated consciousness to evolve the whole. This sea of oneness connects all that is—tree, rock, beast, and human alike. It is that sea that sustains us and gives us life. That same sea also absorbs our life lessons and acquired wisdom as we sink back into it after a lifetime in the desert of incarnation.

In order to do what we need to do, we first need to understand how to tap into this vast sea of energy. Then we need to learn how to shift our center of awareness from the tip of the spike of consciousness in beta to the base of the spike where it interfaces with the great energy sea of awareness in delta. To do that, we need to know what we are looking for and why.

The Evolution of Energy and Consciousness

In the beginning, before there were men, countries, planets, or suns, before even the moment of creation we now know as the big bang, there was a vast, pregnant sea of unrealized potential. Because this pregnant void was the first that had no second, we call it the singularity. From it streamed the essence, or the field, of potential. Before there was the thinnest manifestation on the most ethereal plane, there was this singularity of potential.

The first emanation from this potential we call *universal life-force energy*. It is the knower of the field of potential and, as such, is the all-pervasive undercurrent of all that is to come. It is the divine intelligence, the engine of creation, that drives manifestation. It is the platform upon which the Great Web of Life begins to coalesce. It is also the energy that begins to densify and differentiate in order to create the fundamental energies of the manifest universe, making it the Web's grid as well as the Web's first resident. Undifferentiated universal life-force energy is also the sea of oneness that connects all the residents of the Web of life.

As universal life-force energy continues to densify and differentiate, the different energy layers take shape in the Web. The causal appears, then the subtle, which densifies further into the etheric, until the physical universe comes into being. At this point, the shadings of universal life-force energy have progressed to produce all forms of both subtle and gross matter. These forms, because they have been created from high-powered universal life-force energy, have their own characteristic radiant energy, known as *life-force energy*. Everything in the manifest universe has this energy, from the angels, spirit guides, and devas of the subtle realms down to the sand and pebbles on the beaches of the physical world. It is the energy associated with form. The unique energy that is innate in humans we refer to as *personal life-force energy*.

As we have said, it is the sea of universal life-force energy that sustains us. Every day we need to tap into this source. Just as the physical body requires a recommended daily allowance (RDA) of vitamins and minerals, our energy body requires a daily universal life-force energy allowance (DLFEA). Everyone taps into this energy source automatically during deep, dreamless—delta sleep—and they get what they need to stay alive. But a shaman needs to access this source at will, because personal healing and action in the world and service to the community cannot be undertaken using only personal life-force energy. There just isn't enough of that, and it's for individual use. In order to create balance, harmony, and substantive change, the shaman must learn how to interface with the sea of universal life-force energy in order to plug in and channel that energy for physical-world application.

For one reason or another, we commonly block our connection with universal life-force energy, and we cannot get our DLFEA. When we cannot get our DLFEA, we demonstrate characteristic symptoms of spiritual malaise—symptoms like feeling a spiritual void, the inability to find soul-fulfilling nourishment, gross power/energy loss, low energy, loss of vitality, and a deep dispiritedness that opens the door to opportunistic illness, mental problems, and addictions. In these instances, the personal shaman must be able to tap into the sea of energy and open the door so that the energy can begin to flow within themselves. We usually do this by finding ways to kick-start the energy pump. The first step is for the shaman to shift their center of awareness down to that energy interface at the sea of universal life-force energy. We will cover the finer points of that maneuver in the next chapter, but for now, let's examine ways we can induce reconnection with this high-vibrational energy.

Reconnecting with Universal Life-Force Energy

One of the things shamans notice about themselves when they are having trouble getting their DLFEA is that they are dull. Their aura is not shiny bright, and their vibration is very low. The key to getting reconnected is to remove any blockages, then increase the energy vibration enough that the universal life-force energy can begin to flow freely again. Basically, we can think of this process as clearing the path and then plugging in. You already know how to remove blockages from earlier in this chapter, so let's focus on plugging into that high-vibrational energy.

There are a couple of ways to plug into universal life-force energy. By journeying to the helping spirits and asking for their help, we can immediately accomplish wonders. The spirits are higher-vibration beings swimming in a sea of energy. They will help increase our vibration just by being present with us.

But often, revitalization of a more radical intensity must be employed. In these instances the personal shaman will enter, either in physicality or in journey, a sacred healing-medicine place. There are many of these around the ordinary world and in the Otherworlds. In the ordinary world they are sacred spaces and are known to the locals wherever they are found. The same is true in the Otherworlds, where the helping spirits are the locals. Sitting in the vortex of energy found in a sacred healing-medicine place will allow energy to seep deep into your very being, as if you are soaking in a hot tub of energy. If it is inconvenient to go to one of these spots in physicality, the shaman will journey to one of these places in any of the three worlds and bask in the powerful energy. A sacred healing-medicine place, whether real or imagined, is anywhere you feel whole or where your soul sings. So if you know of no such places in physicality, imagine your own and use it to your advantage.

Another way to induce high-vibrational energy connection is to stimulate yourself with progressively higher-vibrational input until you feel yourself respond. This is the kick-start method. The vibrations employed are color, sound, touch, intention, and energy movement.

Color: The spectrum of energy in color is the same as the visual spectrum. Red is the lowest-energy color vibration, then orange, yellow, green, blue, and indigo; violet is the highest color vibration. One way to increase your vibration level is to visualize each of the chakras, starting at the red root chakra. Feel and see each chakra spinning, healthy and glowing brightly with its characteristic color. See these colors reflected in healthy, radiant boundary layers. See, feel, sense, and experience life-force energy flowing freely into each chakra, and see, feel, sense, and experience the emanations of each of the chakras moving through your energy field. To continue this work, wear higher-vibrational colors during the day, surround yourself with blues and greens in your environment, and continually touch base with these colors in the higher-vibrational spectrum.

Sound: One would think that playing loud, energetic rock and roll might be the answer to increasing vibration using sound. Alas, this is not the case. Loud, three-chord rock is the sonic vibrational equivalent of the orange genital chakra. (Not surprising, huh?) What we need to increase our vibration through sound is sonic stimuli that pull us out of beta and move us deeper into the thinking machinery — the deeper the better. So once again we can use drumming or rattling to bring ourselves to theta or delta frequencies. Chanting, as in kirtans or Gregorian chants, will draw us out of beta and into a higher-vibrational state. Soulful singing is useful, and one of the most effective methods is a technique called toning. Toning can be achieved easily by voicing the syllable *om*. Center yourself, quiet your mind, take a deep breath, and make an *O* sound, allowing the sound to be released as you exhale. Finish with the *M* sound, allowing it to vibrate for as long as you comfortably can until it naturally fades away. Repeat the sound, feeling the vibration fill your chest, then your entire being. There are many CDs on the market that will induce higher vibrations through toning. All of these suggestions open the channels to life-force energy.

Touch: There are a variety of ways to shift vibration through touch. The appropriate method will depend on the personal shaman's preference. Physical touch such as holding your hands or giving yourself a hug can be a simple act with great benefits. You can increase your vibration, as well as release tension, by rubbing your neck, shoulders, or upper back. Consciously moving life-force energy through touch is the next step. Reiki, therapeutic touch, or enhanced massage (massage that includes energy movement) will significantly facilitate an increase in vibration. It is here, through increased vibration, that the shaman can open the door to the sea of life-force energy and begin to thread that energy into themselves.

Intention and Energy Movement: We have already discussed many ways to accomplish energy movement, but the best way to reconnect with universal life-force energy is to journey.

Journeys

Journey to any of the three worlds (unless specified), meet with your soul-self and helping spirits, and do the following:

- Ask to be shown your luminous energy body.

- Explore, learn about, feel, sense, and experience each of your chakras.

- Explore, learn about, feel, sense, and experience each of the layers of your luminous energy body.

- Ask to be shown how and where you spend your personal energy and how you can best save your energy.

- Ask to be shown how you can best increase your energy.

- Ask to be shown how you can stimulate and move personal energy.

- Ask to be shown how you can dissolve energy blockages.

- Ask to be shown how you can seal energy leaks and fortify your energy boundaries.

- Explore and learn about the spiritual and energetic causes and treatments for physical pain and discomfort.

- Journey to the spiritual energies of specific physical ailments, illnesses, diseases, and injuries, such as fatigue, arthritis, Lyme disease, cancer, or fibromyalgia.

- Follow the sensation of physical pain or discomfort all the way down to the core of the issue and ask to be shown the root cause. What does the core feel like inside? What are the messages?

- Explore and learn about the spiritual and energetic causes and treatments for mental pain and discomfort.

- Journey to the spiritual energies of the specific mental ailments and symptoms, such as confusion, mental fog, indecisiveness, or delusion.

- Follow the sensation of mental pain or discomfort all the way down to the core of the issue. What does the core feel like inside? What are the messages?

- Explore and learn about the spiritual and energetic causes and treatments for emotional pain and discomfort.

- Journey to the spiritual energies of the specific mental ailments and symptoms, such as anxiety, depression, panic, dissatisfaction, or emptiness.

- Follow the sensation of emotional pain or discomfort all the way down to the core of the issue. What does the core feel like inside? What are the messages?

- Ask to meet with the helping spirits that will help you remove unwanted or unhealthy energies. How will they help you perform this technique? What will you need to do? What will it be like?

- Ask to meet with the helping spirits that will help you with extraction. How will they help you perform this technique? What will you need to do? What will it be like?

- Journey to a medicine place in the Otherworld and ask your helping spirits to help you perform extraction on yourself.

- Ask to meet with the helping spirits that will help you with dismemberment. How will they help you perform this technique? What will you need to do? What will it be like?

- Journey to a medicine place in the Otherworld and ask your helping spirits to facilitate your dismemberment/shamanic death for healing.

- Ask to be shown, since you understand that energy is everywhere, how you can best redirect energy for your use.

- Ask how to best receive and perceive energy.

- Ask to be given an image, feeling, and sensation for receiving energy, such as a daisy soaking in the sun, a baby robin gulping down its yummy worm breakfast, or the parched earth absorbing raindrops.

- Ask to be shown a sacred healing-medicine place where you can find healing.

Shamans use their own bodies to interact with the energies of others, places, and situations in very conscious ways. Here are three different techniques to explore: puffing up with divine energy, becoming bright and shiny, and becoming diffuse like mist or fog, thinning your form out until you become invisible.

- Make a list of three people you enjoy being with and three people that you do not enjoy being with. Journey to any of the three worlds, meet with your helping spirits, and observe your luminous energy body as it is right then in the journey. Then, one by one, bring each of those six people to you energetically and observe your energy body in connection with theirs. Experiment with how the energies interact, using each of the three energy-changing techniques with each of the six people individually. For example, bring Sally to you and observe your energy body and hers in relation to yours. Now try puffing up with spirit energy and observing how this first affects your energy and then her energy. Notice how you feel and what you feel while doing this. Notice how big your energy is, what color, what texture and consistency, and if there are any holes or dark spots. If so, do those change in size or color, and so on? Relax and allow your energy body to return to normal. Now become as bright and shiny as you possibly can. Observe your energy body and hers in relation to yours. Notice how and what you feel. Relax and allow your energy body to return to normal. Now diffuse your energy into mist until you become invisible. Observe your energy body and hers in relation to yours. Notice how and what you feel. Repeat this process with all six people that you listed.

• List three places where you feel good when you are there and three places that give you the opposite feeling. These do not have to be places that you visit often or know that well. Repeat the journey described above, visiting each of the six places while utilizing each of the three energy-changing techniques. Notice what happens to your luminous energy body when you are in these places and with each technique used. Observe your energy body and the energy of the place. Notice how and what you feel. Repeat this process with all six places that you listed.

• List three situations that make or have made you feel good and three situations that make or have made you feel uncomfortable. Repeat the journey described above, visiting each of the six situations while utilizing each of the three energy-changing techniques. Notice what happens to your luminous energy body when you are in these situations and with each technique used. Observe your energy body and the energy of the place. Notice how and what you feel. Repeat this process with all six situations that you listed.

Journey in any of the three worlds, meet with your helping spirits, and ask to

• Learn about the vibrations and healing power of color and the various colors.

• Learn about the vibrations and healing power of sound and the various sounds.

- Learn about the vibrations and healing power of plants and flowers. Explore specific plants and flowers.

- Learn about the vibrations and healing power of crystals. Explore different kinds of crystals. ·

Exercises: Energy Awareness and Movement

Exercise One: Lighted Energy Egg

The exercise, adapted from Colleen's book *Energy for Life: Connect with the Source*, will light you up, move energy, and help you be more aware of your luminous energy body.

Take in a few deep breaths and shake your shoulders and neck to release any stress or tension from your body. Drum or rattle to shift consciousness and relax your mind. When you feel calm and centered, picture yourself sitting on top of a round rock with a smooth, flat top. The rock is glowing brightly, and when you sit upon it, it makes you light up and glow all over inside. Take a few moments to see, sense, and feel the light glowing through your entire body and energy field. The light inside of you illuminates your energy and looks something like swirling, moist steam wafting up from hot water. Take a few moments to bask in this glow and just observe. You will also be able to easily notice any holes, leaks, and congestion in your luminous energy body. These may appear as spraying energy, empty holes, or dark, dirty or smoky-looking patches. You don't need to do anything about these; just notice them.

Using your will and intention, begin to stimulate your energy field by stirring the energy at your root chakra where you are seated on the lighted rock. After a few moments, send this translucent energy spiraling up the inside of your body. The nourishing energy looks and feels like warm, steamy water bubbling up out of a small internal geyser from your base through the top of your head. Relax and use all of your senses to experience your energy as it continually spirals up your spinal column and billows out through your entire body, clearing away blockages and congestion, sealing leaks, and filling holes. Experience the effervescence of your internal geyser in your body for a few moments. When you are ready, allow it to move into the first layer of your energy field; the energy continues to swirl, clear, seal, and fill. As the energy continues to flow, it grows in strength and dynamism and fills each layer of your energy field, one at a time. As each layer clears and energizes, the energy swirls into each layer until it reaches the outer boundary.

At the outer boundary, an energy membrane surrounds the layers of your energy field, and you feel it thicken and intensify from the power of your gathering personal energies. This luminescent perimeter appears like a flexible, rubbery eggshell that continues to allow the exchange of gases and energy. Inside of your eggshell energy boundary, your body is the yolk, and the layers of your energy field are the white. Reach out and feel the edges of your energy boundary and give your luminous eggshell a color that feels right to you. See, sense, feel, and experience the shell radiating and shimmering in its reclaimed strength and power. This empowered boundary becomes your fortress of protection that allows you to let in and out energy in a healthy way. Inside of your radiant energy boundary, your personal energy nourishes your body and energy field and fills you full of vigor and vitality. You are energized!

Exercise Two: Energy Clearing, Fortifying, and Power-Filling

Take in a few deeps breaths, relax, and drum or rattle for a few moments to shift your consciousness. When you are ready, imagine yourself standing on top of a large cheesecloth of porous, luminescent, divine energy being held at each of the four corners by your helping spirits. Mindfully watch, see, feel, sense, and experience the luminescent energy sheet move up through your feet, legs, torso, arms, shoulders, neck, and head, sifting out all of the dark, congested, and unwanted energies. As they raise it up way over your head, the helping spirits come together in the center of it, joining the corners of the sheet to form a luminescent container for the energies that have been released from your body and energy field. As the energy in the container is released to the universe for transformation, see, sense, and feel yourself clear of walls, dams, and knots that once blocked your energy. See, sense, and watch as the helping spirits surround you in swirling, pulsating rainbow energy until your energy boundaries are fortified and you are filled with vibrant power and energy.

Exercise Three: Receiving Life-Force Energy

This exercise seems too simple to be as powerful as it is. Go into nature, open your mind and heart, and talk with a plant. If you'd like, you can drum, rattle, or sing a bit to help shift your consciousness. Do anything you need to do to relax and open, then simply begin talking with the plant. Be sure to listen as well as talk. You can talk about anything at all. Notice anything and everything that happens both internally and externally. Be sure to thank the plant before you leave. Leave an offering if you'd like. If you didn't bring anything, a personal offering such as a strand of hair is generally acceptable to most nature spirits.

CHAPTER NINE

Energy Liberation and Conservation

Who looks outside, dreams. Who looks inside, awakens.

—Carl Jung

Standing at the campfire, soaking in the intense heat, she feels the energy begin to move within her. Her feet are hip distance apart, her arms are down at her sides, her eyes are closed. With relaxed concentration, she takes in a deep breath and draws in the energy. She peacefully slips into a trance while placing her attention on the soles of her feet and the crown of her head. She feels the strong, grounding energy of the Earth slowly moving up her feet and legs to her root chakra at the base of her spine. Simultaneously, she draws down the universal life-force energy from above and feels it melt in through the top of her head and flow down into her root chakra. Where the two energies meet, her chakra ignites into a vibrant red energy ball that grows and expands, becoming a radiant source of glowing, ruby red light. She feels the light saturating all of the tissues of her body, soaking into her abdomen, chest, and head, and flowing out her arms, bathing organs, muscle, blood, and bone, until her entire body becomes a great neon beacon of light. After a few moments, she intends the ruby energy to recede once again to its home in her base chakra, where it continues to glow and spin brightly.

With relaxed concentration, she takes in a deep breath and draws up the energy from the Earth into her sacral chakra. Simultaneously, she draws down universal life-force energy down through her head and into her sacral chakra. The two energies combine, spin, and glow bright orange. She stirs and expands the energy throughout her body, saturating every cell with this orange, regenerative light. After a few moments, she shrinks the light back to its home in her second chakra, where it continues to spin and glow a brilliant orange.

Using the same technique for each chakra, she power-fills and cleanses her body with the golden energy of her solar plexus chakra, the emerald green of her heart chakra, the azure blue of her throat chakra, the deep purple of her third-eye chakra, and the pale violet of her crown chakra. Each time, she draws the Earth energy up and the universal energy down to create the characteristic spectral light of each chakra. She takes the time to permeate her entire being with each of the energies before moving on to the next.

With all seven chakras energized, continuing to spin and glow in each of their homes, she focuses her attention on the soles of her feet. Taking in a deep breath, she draws up the Earth energy through her feet and legs and into her torso where it mixes with the chakra and life-force energies concentrated in her chakras, forming a swirling, internal rainbow of energy. As it moves through and around her, she feels the rainbow energies saturating, bathing, and cleansing all of her cells. She then draws this rainbow energy up from her feet, through her center, and out the top of her head like a fountain. As the energy exits the crown of her head, she sees the rainbow droplets cascade out to the limits of her aura and down again to her feet. As these rainbow droplets mist through her auric field, she feels her body and her luminescent energy body cleansed and refreshed by the movement of this energy. She keeps the energetic rainbow fountain flowing by focusing her attention on the energy movement until she feels whole, centered, and energized. She leaves the energies flowing as she takes a deep breath and opens her eyes. She knows that energy in motion tends to stay in motion, so the benefits of this exercise will continue as she goes about her daily activities.

Archimedes said, "Give me a lever long enough and a fulcrum on which to place it, and I shall move the world." What he was talking about was the proper application of energy to create a shift. But in order to create a shift, in order to make a difference, the energy must be available, and in order for there to be a shift of any kind, the difference must be observable. Nothing observable—no difference. Unfortunately, many people live lives that display no difference for days or even years at a time. It is interesting to observe, quite shamanically, that the ultimate state where there is never a difference made is death. Which brings us to the most brutally honest realization in shamanism: if you aren't making a difference, you are already dead—plain and simple. It doesn't matter what's coming. It doesn't matter what must be done or can be done. You've already checked out, so how bad can what's to come be, really?

But it doesn't need to be that way at all. You just need the energy to shift.

So far, we have discussed the nature of the thinking machinery, cultivating awareness, the elements of power, how to visualize healing, and what energy is and how it works. We have learned the sacred technology of journeying and how to utilize and cultivate that art to make a difference. This body of information is one side of the shamanic coin. It is referred to collectively as *dreaming.*

The other side of that same coin is how to reclaim lost energy from our past and clear away enough of our personal issues to allow the soul to express itself. How, exactly, do we free ourselves enough so that clarity becomes our constant companion? How do we free energy trapped in our past, find the life-forming beliefs that originate in our earliest life experiences, then rewrite them so they no longer sabotage us? The techniques we can use to address these concerns are referred to as *stalking.*

Dreaming and Stalking

As unfortunate as these names may be, *dreaming* and *stalking* are the traditional terms referring to two distinct ways the soul functions in the world. Dreaming should not be confused with what we do during sleep at night. This term, used in this context, refers to shamanic dreaming and represents a more specific function than the flights of fancy we take during sleep. The term *stalking* may be even more misleading. It is decidedly not referring to an obsessive skill used to invade the privacy of a celebrity. When we refer to shamanic stalking, what we mean is the way that energies and intent are harnessed and directed to make the needed changes that allow us to precipitate the manifestation of a new reality.

Everyone knows someone who has a natural skill for storytelling. It seems like they can relate a tale so as to make you perfectly understand and viscerally experience what it is they are describing or relating. Perhaps you know someone you work with who everyone thinks of as "the idea person." They have uncanny vision into a concept or an idea and are able to convey this vision to others through their communication. Maybe you know someone who has the near-prescient ability to see into a problem, being able to dissect each nuance of the problem's origins and ultimate effects. Or maybe you have been exposed to a mother or a father who was able to close their eyes and focus in on their absent children and be able to tell if they are okay and behaving themselves.

These are all typical examples of dreaming. A dreamer can see into the potential of things or understand a concept so thoroughly that it nearly seems to be part of them. Dreamers are the idea people, the visionaries, the seers, and the ones who can envision a potential reality.

Conversely, maybe you are acquainted with someone else who knows how to get things done. They seem to be able to connect the dots in order to bring a project to fruition. If you describe something to them that you need to accomplish, they can tell you whom to talk to, what you will need, and the sequence that you must employ in order to get the task done. These people are the stalkers. They are the doers, the movers and shakers, and ones who know how to make things happen.

In this way, we can see that the dreamers and stalkers represent a hand-in-glove relationship. We need people who can cook up an idea and other people who can serve it up. We need concept and process, idea and method, form and function, the "know-what" and the "know-how." Everyone in the world has a particular tendency towards either stalking or dreaming. Everyone has skills for both, but generally speaking, each of us has a propensity towards one or the other. It is rare for someone to be a pure dreamer who has no stalker ability, or to be a pure stalker with no dreamer ability. But it doesn't take dreaming ability to realize that great things can be done when dreaming and stalking are combined to achieve a specific end.

Dreaming and stalking, used in tandem, are the one-two punch of creation. If you look at any company that offers a product or service, there are always departments that specialize in dreaming, such as Research and Development; then there are departments that specialize in stalking, such as Manufacturing and Marketing. The two combined shift reality. Where once there was nothing but unrealized potential, dreaming and stalking work together to create something that has never existed before or manage to change what is into what can be. This creation is a product of the Agreement between the two.

Agreement is capitalized here to indicate a shamanic Agreement, which is fundamentally different from an ordinary agreement. Shamanic Agreements are forged at the soul level and require all parties to clearly express their soul's intent and put their life on the line to change the nature of reality by making a difference. Many ordinary agreements change nothing. The parties involved are in the same situation, frame of mind, or position at the end of the agreement event as they were at the beginning. The beginning and ending of a shamanic Agreement event are never the same. There are no head-nod or "we'll see" agreements within the shamanic Agreement framework. A shamanic Agreement brings about a prespecified change based on the terms of the Agreement. No change indicates no Agreement.

In spite of the real-world examples we have mentioned, dreaming and stalking are functions of the soul. They are natural expressions of our individual spiritual skill sets and can be thought of as intuitive skills. In other words, they arise from us without undue thought. Dreams spring into the mind of a dreamer like water flowing into a cup. Methodologies and techniques soak into the mind of a stalker like sunshine on rich earth. From these two, the seed of potential can blossom into the flower of change.

How do we use these expressions to our advantage as personal shamans? The first thing we need to know is what we are after.

Setting the Stage with Dreaming

As we have said, if we are going to be of any value whatsoever to ourselves and our communities as shamans, we need to clear a pathway from our soul to our conscious mind. In order to do this, we will first need to figure out what is in the way, and to do that, we need to see into ourselves using both dreaming and stalking. Ideally, what we want to do is shift the center of our awareness from beta/conscious thinking to delta/soul-based awareness. When we drop our awareness down to delta, we effectively step out of the programs and points of view we are unconsciously running and that sabotage our best intentions and cause us pain. We gain perspective on what programs, behaviors, and beliefs stand in the way between our soul and its free expression into the outside world.

Unfortunately, the same stuff that stands in the way of the soul expressing itself from down below stands between those who attempt to descend from beta consciousness up above. So we as personal shamans must approach this work with dedication and tenacity, being willing to release everything to which we are attached and to examine the nature of what we believe and why. Without that detachment, we merely reprogram the very things we are attempting to remove.

Dreaming in the form of journeying is how we propose you do research, so the work you will do when you stalk yourself is effective. Mindful bare awareness must be employed during these journey sessions. As shaman for yourself, you must be willing to look unflinchingly at the places you might rather avoid.

Initially, we recommend you journey to look into the world around you and how you relate to it and how others relate to you. Journey to see if you can notice any patterns or repeating scenarios in these relationships. These will appear to you as you examine the larger tapestry of your interactions with the world around you. Perhaps when you look at your career, you can see things you do repeatedly that do not serve you. Ask your helping spirits to assist you in these exploratory journeys because you cannot always see what you are in the middle of doing. Remember, you can't see the color of your own eyes without a mirror. In this case, your helping spirits serve as your mirror, showing you what you do and how you do it. Make a note of the patterns you discover during these journeys.

Now employ these same techniques to an examination of your inner world. Using journeying, look at your energy body and see if there are energy filaments dragging behind you, linking you to events in your past. Play back the memories of your life and examine them. See if, as you review your life, you come across hot spots still bursting with unresolved emotions. As you come across these spots, make note of them without judgment. You will come back to them when you stalk yourself. When you remember certain memories, are there times you get flashes of anger, resentment, fear, or overwhelming regret? Make note of these hot spots. It may serve you to keep a pad and pen next to you as you journey, so that you can jot down this information as you discover it, but avoid taking detailed notes while in journey. Just jot down a key word to use as a mnemonic device. Then once you have come out of the journey, you can take further notes on that memory. These notes will help you with your next step as you being the work of stalking yourself.

Stalking Yourself

Every stalk has a purpose, an intent, that guides it. Certain stalks are orchestrated by the soul, and you do not have to be conscious of the intent in order for the outcome of a stalk to be favorable. Many everyday life "coincidences" are examples of soul-orchestrated stalks.

For example, the new age has coined the phrase "when the student is ready, the teacher will appear." What is happening here is that the student begins to stalk herself to prepare for instruction by processing personal issues and becoming aware of areas in her life that need to change. This personal stalk occurs on all the different levels of consciousness, originating from the soul. At the same time the student is stalking herself, she is moving herself into harmony with the teacher, in essence stalking her. So when the student is ready, the teacher who is ready for a student and who has likely been stalking students appears. Seems like magic, but it's just simple energetics.

Many coincidences follow these same mechanics. We are guided by our soul to seek out and find what we need in order to fulfill our soul agenda. This may or may not be a conscious process. But it's still a stalk. For our purpose, the intent to clear away our personal history is the one we will use as we do this work.

Erasing personal history may sound a bit ominous, but it is a purely logical explanation of the work we must do to clear that soul/mind pathway. Think about it. There is no other moment than the present one. No matter how hard we try, we will not be able to live in any other moment than the one we are in right now. But often we get pulled away from the present moment and into a world of illusion within our own minds. We find ourselves dealing with what we are supposed to be doing (conditioning), what happened the last time this situation came up (past memories), what we always do in these situations (behavioral programs), or our strong emotional reactions (theta programs). All these—conditioning, memories, and programs—are parts of our personal history that interfere with our ability to truly live in the present moment. They are distractions, illusions that steal our lives away from us, and by dismantling them, we find ourselves back in the present moment. In so doing, we also gain a clear pathway through our thinking machinery. Not only do we get to live our lives engaged in the present moment, but we also are then able to express our soul into the world in real time, with no gap between the impulse to express our soul and the expression itself. Instantaneous, authentic soul expression is the goal of the shaman.

Once you have set the stage by dreaming/journeying to examine your inner and outer worlds, then you are ready to begin the intensive work of stalking yourself. One of the most focused and effective ways to do this is to map out a timeline of your life. We have found it useful to use graph paper, designating each square as a year, or to use notebook paper vertically, setting aside several lines between years so that you have room to write memories or emotional information as you perform your stalk. Begin with your earliest memories. Include even the stories your family has told you about the time before you can remember. Everything you can recall is important, especially from birth to age twenty-one, but recall everything for the entirety of your life. If you are one of the fortunate few who have an eidetic memory, just record the events that stand out for you. Remembering what you had for breakfast every morning growing up is unnecessary. But then, if you received a gold star for eating your fruit one day or a beating because you wouldn't eat breakfast one morning when you were nine years old, by all means write that down.

Your timeline is likely to take some time. You may want to use multiple journeys, as well as memory, to help you finish it all the way through to the present.

Once you have your life's timeline complete, examine it. Do you find patterns emerging during this examination? Write those down. Do you find recurring emotions cropping up for you? Recurring behaviors? Make a note of them, perhaps marking the recurring similar emotions with a red star and the recurring behaviors with a blue star. Be very detailed in this emotional and behavioral analysis. Track down and identify distressful emotions like worry, depression, anxiety, panic attacks, anger, rage, or fear. Strong emotions such as these are important clues to what is going on inside of you. They act as an internal fire alarm, flashing a warning from your soul-self to your conscious mind to indicate that there is a conflict between what is really true in objective reality and what you believe to be true and how you are living your life. Strong emotions are our natural fight-or-flight response to subtle or overt confrontation between truth and illusion.

For example, if a person believes that he must be strong and in charge of what goes on in his life at all times, even the simple act of riding as a passenger in a car can challenge his beliefs. The objective reality is that someone else can drive and that he does not have to be in charge in that moment. However, his belief tells him unconsciously that something is wrong because he is not in charge. As his "control" program is triggered, he begins to feel anxious, so he criticizes the driver's driving abilities. The driver responds by asking him why he is being so critical, and he explodes with anger. He is ready to fight. Another person in the same situation might respond to the question by becoming depressed, sullen, and pouty—ready to flee and retreat. It is very important to find these trigger points in yourself by sifting through your timeline, keeping an eye out for emotional responses and behavioral patterns, and asking yourself, "What am I making real?"

Additionally, you will want to look for indications of physical imbalances. Do you find recurring illnesses? When did these occur? Did they happen in or around other events of note? Are those events similar to each other? Are these connected with any emotional responses or behavioral patterns?

Also, make note of recurring healthy emotions, behaviors, or trends that you have habitually performed. Make note of the very positive memories you have, examining what makes them wonderful for you.

Take the time to examine the types of relationships and agreements you have made in your life. Are your relationships healthy and satisfying? If not, why? When you made agreements were you able to keep them once you had made them? Do you have a tendency to make the same agreements over and over? Do you obligate yourself in the same way for the same reasons time and again? Make a note of these agreements, the occasions on which you've made them, and the circumstances under which you make them.

Once you have examined your life and made note of all the recurring behaviors, emotions, illnesses, issues, and agreements, focus your attention on the period from birth through age four. We know that this period of time is when you set your beliefs in place. Everything that came later in life will have been built on these early beliefs. Close examination will reveal that nearly all of your patterned behaviors will find their way back to an incipient event that occurred between birth and age four. Journey on this seminal event, taking the time to identify what happened back then. Are you able to see the roots of your lifelong behaviors in those earliest days of your life? Do not be alarmed if you cannot. Sometimes these connections take some time to present themselves. But pursue them until they are revealed. When you can see an event that seems to be at the root of many of your behaviors, ask your helping spirits to show you the nature of the belief you put in place then. That belief is the keystone upon which your lifelong behaviors and programs are built.

We know a gentleman who had spent his entire life just scraping by. He was brilliant, but he had several behaviors in place that continually defeated him. He had a deeply engrained problem with authority and would fight it tooth and nail. He also had an issue with self-esteem, stemming in part from the fact he was morbidly obese. When he came for help, he knew something was wrong, because he had done everything he could to lose the weight, but nothing he did helped. He did the work surrounding his timeline and discovered a memory of his father force-feeding him in his highchair. His father would put in a spoonful of baby food, and this little boy would spit it out. His father would once again scrape it up and feed it to the baby, and once again the baby spit it out. This continued for several hours until the baby had been forced to eat every bit of that baby food. Much wailing and trauma had ensued during the process — so much so, in fact, that the fellow's older siblings had run and hid in their rooms until it was all over. This single event had set this man up for several of his lifelong programs. One was that food was love. Too much food and overfeeding represented *lots* of love. Another program put in place by the highchair event was the following: "You can't tell me what to do. I know you will try, but I won't do it, even though I know I will get into *big* trouble, and even though I know you will win in the end." This program was part and parcel of his authority issues and the losing struggle with authority that he always seemed to be embroiled in. The final belief, and the biggest one, was that he was a screw-up. He believed on a very deep level that he could not be trusted to know what was right for him. This belief manifested the life he was leading. Although a very bright fellow, he would catastrophically sabotage his opportunities because at his deepest level, he believed he was going to screw up everything anyway. It was a self-fulfilling prophecy. His entire life was being orchestrated by a two-year-old in a highchair.

To remedy these programs and beliefs, he began the journey-work and undertook the intensive examination of his life and his lifelong patterns. Using the technique described in the next section, he journeyed to retrieve the energy locked up in events throughout his life, and he used that energy to rewrite those early beliefs that had plagued him. Once the beliefs were rewritten, the programs that proceeded from them fell away. Today, this gentleman has found his way into a new profession, stopped getting himself into trouble with authority, and lost his excess weight. Once he realized what had been going on and addressed the anger surrounding that, he told us the weight just dropped off him. He was flabbergasted, but delighted. The same is true for anyone who does the work, because life shifts to reflect held beliefs. Rewrite the beliefs, rewrite the life.

Recapitulation and Energy Reclamation

The first step in erasing your personal history, clearing your pathway, and rewriting your beliefs is to reclaim the energy you have locked in the events of your life (Reclamation). Now is when you put to use all of that hard work you did on your timeline analysis. Through repeated journeys, go back to the events of your life where there is trauma or lingering emotion. Re-enter the event, and while there, consciously release your attachment to the event and the consequences of the event (Recapitulation). Focus on whatever energy you may have lost or that may be caught there for you. This energy is pure life-force energy, not traumatized emotional energy. Collect it and reabsorb it into yourself, consciously seeing it come back to you (Reclamation). Cut the energy filament or cord which may be attached to that event. If other people are involved, release them, see them releasing you, give back to them what energy is theirs (Recapitulation), and reclaim from them what energy is yours (Reclamation).

Repeat this process for every significant event in your life, positive or negative. See, feel, and experience these events as objectively as you can. Ask yourself, "What am I making real?" Track down, identify, and release those recurring distressing emotions, drawing the energy locked up in them and in the events that precipitate them. Track down, identify, and release recurring unhealthy thoughts and behaviors, drawing the energy back to you that is locked up in them and in the events associated with them. Track down, identify, and release all of the spots where you were hurt or mistreated, or perceived that you were. Track down, identify, and release situations where you missed the mark, where you were caught in ego or self-involvement, and collect the energy that is yours from those instances. Track down, identify, and release all of the unhealthy agreements you have made to the detriment of yourself and others. Untie those knots of obligation and reclaim the energy tied up in them. Again, since others will be involved, release them and see them releasing you. Give back to them what is theirs and reclaim from them what is yours.

Now journey to the places where you were brilliant. Pull that energy out of those places and add that to your present moment. Journey to the healthy emotions, healthy recurring thoughts and behaviors, and the places where you did hit the mark, and draw the strength, power, and energy inherent in those instances back into yourself. As with their unhealthy cousins, cut the energy filaments and cords that may be attached to these events as well. Mark the feelings of the success of those moments, but release them nonetheless. You need not live in the past to feel that triumph. You will be creating that in the present now.

Reassimilate all these energies into yourself. Once you have done so, journey to the earliest events and focus your now highly empowered intent to shift the old beliefs that have created the behaviors that stand in your way. Ask to be shown what is real and what is an illusion created by your thoughts, emotions, or perceptions. Release them and see them disappear. Rewrite them, if necessary, and see them changed to beliefs that do serve you and that are advantageous for you and your community. See yourself as the soul you are, moving and acting in the world according to your unique soul path. Without the shackles of your harmful beliefs and behaviors, are you able to see your soul's expression? Can you see now, looking at the positive inclinations and behaviors you have exhibited throughout your personal history, what you have been trying to do your entire life? You will likely see a pattern. This is the signature of the soul's expression. Cultivate it and nurture it, for it is your destiny.

When you have done all of this, reexamine your energy body. If there are any filaments still dragging behind you or cords attached to you, stalk them. Follow them all the way back to where they lead and perform the reclamation and recapitulation exercises you need to reclaim that energy. This cleanup may take months as the old falls away and you are able to mop up the last of the trapped energy. Don't rush it. Be patient and enjoy the present moment, pursuing this work further when presented with something that pulls you out of the present moment. Your awareness will now be keen to these instances, so when one occurs, stalk it as you have stalked all the others, reclaiming what is yours.

Reclamation and recapitulation are highly useful tools for integrating the self. Often, though, it is difficult to see all the places you might be caught in your programming or personal history. In these instances, it is recommended that you work with someone trained in the methodology of self-integration and expression of the soul through the body. (If you are interested in assistance, we recommend visiting *www.TheOtherForum.net,*) where you will find contact information for shamanic practitioners.

Ongoing Work and Special Considerations

During and shortly after the recapitulation and reclamation process, it is quite common for people to feel a lot of different and ofttimes confusing feelings, which they have a difficult time understanding, explaining, and coping with. Many people feel light, free, and happy, yet sad, angry, and bewildered, all at the same time. Some people feel these feelings subtly, while others feel them intensely. When you think about it, it's not surprising that these mixed feelings would occur, since the purpose of the recapitulation and reclamation process is to erase the old reality and create a new one. This kind of change is likely to bring about some fears, defenses, and adjustment issues for most people.

One of the most common unpleasant feelings that people describe is feeling lost. This feeling is very understandable, given the nature of the process. Prior to the recapitulation and reclamation process, our lives and realities have been built upon beliefs, programs, patterns, looping tapes, and conditioning that may or may not have served us well. In our healing process we have examined these and likely released many of them or are in the process of doing so. This release of old programs could leave us feeling like we don't know who we are and that we have no foundation to stand upon. This feeling of "going with the flow" and "living from the soul" is fluid and can feel a bit soft and squishy—so much so that sometimes it can elicit fear of loss of control and instability. It's like we have gone from standing on the Earth to free-falling through the sky.

This feeling may be difficult, but we encourage you not to do anything to "fix" it. You, and it, are not broken. There is nothing to fix and nothing that needs to be changed. Instead, we encourage you to take a deep breath, accept it, and perhaps even enjoy it. This experience can be a very freeing, and if, through conscious choice and intent, you are able to release any anxieties or fears that crop up, continuing to flow with your newfound fluidity, you will find it to be quite joyful.

Another spot where people are sometimes challenged after the initial reclamation and recapitulation process is grief. Grief can stem from many different sources, but it almost always feels devastating and is a potential source of significant energy loss. Meditation on this grief will show you that it is a natural part of releasing old programs. Nature shows us that everything has a beginning, a life, and an end. For people, that cycle corresponds to birth, life, and death. This cycle happens to us all and to everything in this world of impermanence. But endings have a tendency to bring up all kinds of behaviors, programs, and beliefs we didn't even know we had or were a part of us. The reactions we demonstrate at endings are a product of our attachments. These attachments are illusions, but they hurt when they are severed. Grief is a natural reaction to these severings and should be approached with understanding and compassion. It is healthy to mourn what we have lost and the absences we feel, but we must also observe ourselves in these moments of loss. What are we holding onto that can hurt us? Where is it we find ourselves when what has been known is released or rewritten? What beliefs come up that we need to address and adjust?

It is important to process the emotions and grief so that you do not get caught in them. There is an exercise at the end of this chapter for doing just that. But once the grief is processed, it's important to examine the reality. The truth is, you are the same soul, on the same path, before your loss as you are after it. Indeed, the experience of your loss may sharpen your understanding of your destiny, your life purpose, your soul path. In these moments, seek out agreements that feed this purpose. Allow the event of loss to galvanize you to renewed fervor to express your soul in the world. We all may experience loss during this and the coming age, but if we see it as an opportunity, rather than a catastrophe, we will make that difference we seek.

This period of mopping up is a great time to make new agreements that will serve you. Speak with your friends and tell them about the work you have done and are doing on yourself and encourage them to tell you the truth about what they see in you. Sometimes, the people around you know you better than you know yourself. They may open further opportunities for you to reclaim energy and re-adjust old beliefs and programming that you were unable to see by yourself. Stay open and understanding, humble and spirit engaged. Encourage your friends to tell it to you straight and be brutally hon-est with you, so that you can hold yourself in the new reality and stay in the present moment. By setting up a strategic network of people in agreement with you about embracing the new reality and releasing the old one, you energize what you want and further dis-tance yourself from what you do not.

Our clarity is what allows us to be shamans. Our ability to cut through illusion makes us shamans. Our determination to stay en-gaged in the present moment and express our soul's intent, even while in the trenches, makes us shamans. Our practice of using the world as a mirror so we can reflect back the truth makes us shamans. Our ability to see into the other worlds and bring back help and en-ergy from beings and planes of higher vibration makes us shamans. Shifting our awareness out of beta and down to delta makes us sha-mans. Seeing the soul of the world in every rock, stream, bird, and cloud makes us shamans.

But beyond that, beyond all the skills and orientations and per-ceptions and techniques, what makes us shamans is the fact that we are dedicated to using all that we are, all that we have, and all that we were ever meant to be in order to make a positive difference in the world. That intent, that collective agreement, in and of itself, is enough to shift our reality out of the depths of the Kali Yuga and toward brighter days ahead. It is the shamanism of agreement that will distinguish us in the days and years of the coming age. Embrace that, and the future must conform to our belief. After all, hasn't it always?

Journeys

Journey to any of the three worlds (unless specified), meet with your soul-self and helping spirits, and do the following:

- Ask the helping spirits to teach you shamanic dreaming.

- Ask the helping spirits to teach you about shamanic stalking.

- Ask to be shown how you can clear the pathway from your soul to your consciousness in your daily practice and everyday life.

- Ask for assistance from your helping spirits to do some clearing now, in this journey.

- Ask for insight into your personal thinking machinery. Learn about delta, theta, alpha, and beta and what each of these feels like for you.

- Explore and learn about perceptions. What are they? How do they help us? How do they limit us? Ask to be shown your perceptions.

- Ask to be shown the way that you see the world.

- Ask to be shown your opinions and judgments of yourself, others, and the world.

- Ask to be shown your strengths and how to utilize them in advantageous ways.

- Ask to be shown your programs and conditionings and ways that you can clear or rewrite those that do not serve you.

- Ask to be shown how others see you.

- Merge with a helping spirit and see yourself through its eyes.

- Ask to be shown your luminous energy body and the energy filaments dragging behind you that keep you attached to the past. What are they attached to? Don't do anything right now; just observe and see as many as you can—all if possible.

- Revisit the last journey and ask to be shown one energy filament that is dragging behind you, holding you back. Don't
  do anything with it yet; simply explore and learn all you can
  about it. Hear the story, see what is does, how it works, and
  in what ways it limits you.

- Revisit this journey again and ask what you can do to release that filament—cut it, pull it out, dissolve it, make a
  new agreement, make a lifestyle change. Do it in the journey
  if appropriate; if not, begin the process as soon as you can
  after the journey.

- Step outside of yourself and look back. Ask to be shown
  what you look like and how you behave when you are living and expressing yourself from your soul. Pay attention,
  observe. Then examine how you behave when you are living
  your programs. Be objective and unemotionally involved.
  Accept—don't defend. Be a detective—investigate. Don't
  fix—find.

- Ask to be shown when, where, and how this program was
  written. Where is the origin, the starting point, the core trigger? Did you take on something that was someone else's,
  such as their belief or point of view? Did you adopt a different way of being, such as putting on a mask or taking on an
  artificial identity? Did you lose energy or a part of yourself?
  Don't correct it, just observe.

- Ask what this program means to and for you. How has
  it affected you through your life? How does it affect you
  now? Don't do anything to fix it; just listen and watch.
  Learn from it.

- Return to the journey and ask for spirit assistance to reca-
  pitulate and reclaim the energies, releasing what no longer
  serves you and reclaiming what belongs to you that was lost.
  Ask what you need to do in your life to delete or rewrite this

program. What will you do with this returned energy and released block?

- Ask to learn how to live from your soul center. Ask your helping spirits and soul-self to alert you when a program is running so you can live from the soul all the time, and also so you can become aware of the program and rewrite it.

- Ask to be shown what you believe about power, personal power, and the use of power. Release your point of view, your judgments, and what you think you know. Ask the helping spirits, "What is power?" Where does power come from? What is the source?

- Ask to be shown where, when, why, and how you have lost power.

- Ask to be shown where, when, why, and how you stand in your power.

- Ask to be shown where you hold or channel power in your body and energy field.

- Ask to be shown how power and energy are garnered, lost, and exchanged in agreement—and in disagreement. What happens to your energy field in each case?

- Ask to be shown a time that you have "cursed" yourself with a thought, feeling, or statement that binds or limits you in some way. Learn about the event. Then take the power and energy out of it by intentionally pulling the life-force energy and your personal power out of the event. Reclaim the energy and release the event.

- Reclaim the life-force energy and your personal power out of an unrealized dream or opportunity.

- Ask what you can do to be power filled and powerful 24/7/365.

Exercises: Energy Movement and Liberation

Exercise One: Recapitulation and Reclamation

The following exercise has been adapted from Colleen Deatsman's book *Inner Power: Six Techniques for Increased Energy and Self-Healing.*[x]

Make yourself comfortable in your soft space and put on some soothing music. Take some deep breaths and drum or rattle for a few minutes to shift consciousness. Sit quietly and allow the memory of an event or situation that bothers you and won't seem to go away to come to mind. Utilize your truth spot, felt sense, and the inner wisdom of your soul-self to ask and answer these questions with sincere honesty:

- Why do I think that this situation is still emotionally charged for me?

- What emotions stand out initially?

- Looking underneath these initial reactions at the dynamics of the entire situation, what do I feel? What do I think?

- Does this situation challenge the way I think things should be?

- What are my beliefs that hold this view in place?

- What happened that I can't get past?

- What part of myself did I leave behind?

- Did I give a part of myself to another person? If yes, who? How? Why?

- Is there something that attached itself to me during the course of this situation? If yes, what? From whom or where? How and why?

- Is there something that I took from this situation or another person? If yes, what? From whom and where? How and why?

- Is there a part of myself still trapped in this situation? If yes, what part? Where and how is this part trapped? What does this part feel like?

Continuing to stand openly and honestly inside of the situation, reach out and pick up the energy that you lost and reinternalize it by using the strength of your will. Sit openly in this situation and feel the energy of you—not your thoughts or emotions or the thoughts or emotions of another, but the energy of you. This energy is usually felt with your energy field, and it often feels like a warm familiarity that resonates with the inside of your body. This energy may be a little foreign at first, but as you focus and allow yourself to feel, you will notice it. When you do, powerfully take back this energy that is yours by feeling and visualizing it leaving the situation and coming back into you. It may look and feel like the old you, or it may look and feel different. Either way, it's you. This energy is yours and has always been yours, so take it back.

Continuing to stand openly and honestly inside of the situation, see, feel, and sense what attached to you or what you captured in this situation that is decidedly not yours, and use your will to remove it. Visualize and fully feel the entire situation and all of the energies involved. Feel it surrounding you as if you were wearing it like an old coat. Feel the color, the weight, and the texture. Feel the energies, the words, and the emotions. Make sure that you really feel it, and then take off this old coat that weighs you down. Wriggle right out of it like a snake shedding its old skin. Scoop it out, brush it off, and use your will to send it back. Be done with it. In this case, it's *not* yours. Give it up! Send it home and be done with it. Notice how much lighter and freer you feel. Journal your experience.

Exercise Two: Removal

Choose a program, behavior, or identity that you would like to remove or release. Think about it, feel it, see it, journey on it, write about it, explore it, and learn all that you can about it. Learn such things as where it came from, how it has shaped you and your life, how it continues to affect you now, and why it is still with you. When you have thoroughly explored it, energetically pour all of the feelings, thoughts, and findings into an article of clothing, such as a vest, button-down shirt, or jacket. Put on the object and wear it, noticing how it affects your actions, thoughts, and feelings. The longer you can wear the item, the more you will learn about the program and yourself. When you are ready to release the program, stand in front of a full-length mirror and with reverence and conscious awareness take the article of clothing off. Notice anything and everything that you experience. Look in the mirror and see who you are without this program. Wash the article of clothing and notice the cleansing effects of this exercise.

Exercise Three: Grief Ceremony

The purpose of this ceremony is to recall, regurgitate, and release all the emotions and grief you can feel for everything that is, was, and will be—your losses, anxieties, sadnesses, hurt feelings, societal oppression, the hurt of the Earth and her people, the plants, the animals, the trees, our ignorance, our traumas, our victimizations, and our afflictions toward others. Grief is a powerful release of the emotions that may arise during the recapitulation and reclamation process, and those emotions that you knowingly and unknowingly carry around day-to-day and that create pain in your body and mind.

Begin by creating a ceremonial altar for your grief offering. This altar can be made of anything that feels right for you—perhaps a blue cloth representing free-flowing emotional waters, and other symbols or objects representing some things that you know you would like to grieve for.

When you are ready, drum, rattle, or sing for a few moments to shift your consciousness. You may find it helpful to listen to sad, philosophical music that is sure to evoke your deepest emotions. Either sitting in silence or listening to the music, begin to allow yourself to think about and feel all the pain in your life. If your body hurts, feel it. If you feel angry or depressed, feel it. Let yourself feel it all, fully and deeply. You may even notice a deep sadness about everything and nothing in particular, or feel so world-weary that you don't want to struggle with your issues or healing path anymore. Allow yourself to fill with emotion and vulnerability, then let yourself scream and cry—releasing it all, letting it all go. This release is the intention of the ceremony. Swell up inside with anger, frustration, fear, depression, sadness, anxiety, emptiness, confinement, and whatever else flows in, and then let those emotions pour out of you, again and again. Scream, yell, and cry with all of your heart and soul. If you get angry, punch a pillow, or if you feel sad, cry until your guts hurt. Whatever the feelings and reactions, let them flow without judgment. Release, release, release, and then release even more, with wild abandon.

As you finish purging, notice if you feel any lighter. Take the time to examine how you feel about reality once the emotional load is relieved. Can you feel the freedom and clarity inherent in the post-purge event? Can you see who you truly are when not weighed down by grief and disappointment? Can you now see your path before you?

Exercise Four: Rainbow Fountain

The story at the beginning of this chapter describes the power of the Rainbow Fountain exercise. Reread the story, imagining yourself as the practitioner, and then set the book aside and perform the exercise. Feel the energy, feel the colors, and feel the power.

CHAPTER TEN

Living the Shamanic Life

The people who are trying to make this world worse are not taking a day off.
How can I? Light up the darkness!

—Bob Marley

She danced and danced and danced, like she had never danced before. A wild kaleidoscope of flowing colors made her gauze dress look like the pulsating wonder of the aurora borealis. Round and round and round she swirled, losing herself so completely in the rhythm and words she felt herself become each being of the song—just a bag of bones and then the energy of all things.

I am the river, I am the sea,
I am the forest, I am the tree,
I am the mountain, I am the stone,
I am the desert, I am the bone,

We dance in circles around and around
We dance in circles around and around

I am the elder, I am the new,
I am the nation, I am you,
I walk a fine line, I run with wolves,
I fly with eagles, I dance with fools,

I laugh in silence, I cry out loud,
I scream in anger, I stand too proud,
I am the mountain, I am the stone,
I am the desert, I am the bone,

We dance in circles around and around
We dance in circles around and around
We dance in circles around and around
We dance in circles around and around

"Circles," Barb Barton[xi]

As this sacred song so beautifully expresses, we are not only who we think we are—we are also all things, and all things are us, amalgamated, circling, and cycling through this experience we call life. In fact, there is a universal law that speaks to this understanding: as above, so below; as within, so without. Indeed, this principle is what your personal medicine wheel is all about. We are individual and collective all at the same time. This belief is not unique to shamanism, but is an understanding whose time has come. It was exciting for us to see that physicist Dr. Garrett Lisi recently presented this concept to the scientific world in his E8 Uber Theory of Everything.[xii] Lisi is attempting to quantify for the modern world something that shamans have known for thousands of years—separateness is an illusion, a trick of the consciousness and the programming of our life experiences, culture, times, and level of awareness. This illusion of separation makes us think that we are an island, unaffected by what goes on around us and not responsible for what we think and do. This dangerous trick can adversely affect others with whom we share the planet and our lives, and leave us feeling lonely, empty, and dissatisfied without knowing why. In our not so distant past and still today in many subcultures, clans and tribes operate as a single unit focused on the survival and good of "the people." Individual accomplishments are celebrated, tragedies are shared, and villages split workloads, raise children together, and learn from the elders that they care for. We have a lot to learn from these communal versus individual bands; the people know that they share energy and that the same energy that pops tree buds open into sun-gathering leaves and guides the beaver to craft his dam also courses within and through us all. The people know that what happens to one person happens to us all and that what we do to the Earth, we do to ourselves.

Shamans understand and operate from the precept that we are all One. Not only are we not separate from one another or from nature, but we are also not separate within ourselves. We are a soul, body, and mind that must work in unison, not as separate parts. Modern Western culture is the "I" culture. We are taught to focus on ourselves and get as far ahead as we can. To do this, we learn to use our minds and believe that what we think is not only real, but it is also the only way.

All spiritual paths of the world have this one thing in common — unification of body, mind, and spirit. What this means to a personal shamanic practitioner is that we must work diligently to embody, embrace, and express this concept in our life, both internally and externally. Internally, we must integrate mind, body, and soul, and externally we must express this integrated self in the world as a cog in the wheel of the wholeness of everything. So let's get started. Shamanic living begins within the self. Perhaps this well-known story will help you continue looking within.

A grandfather was talking to his grandson about how he felt. He said, "I feel as if I have two wolves fighting in my heart. One wolf is the vengeful, angry, violent one. The other is the loving, compassionate one." The grandson asked him, "Which wolf will win the fight in your heart?" The grandfather answered, "The one I feed."

Which wolf will you choose to feed? If you feed the wolf of suffering by maintaining the imbalances or behaviors that keep them in place, this wolf will win over the wolf of vibrant living. Ultimately, the choice is yours. The results rest in the fortitude of your own intent.

If you choose the wolf of vibrant living, a daily spiritual practice, such as journeying, is the first step to living life in a shamanic way. We can't stress this strongly enough. The work that you do for and within yourself creates the you that shines out into the world. If you want to be a healthy, joyful, well-balanced person in your everyday life, you will need to do your inner work to be that person. At times living shamanically will be the hardest thing you'll ever have to do. Other times it will be the easiest, most natural thing. Always, it ends up being the best thing you can do for yourself.

Personal Spiritual Practice

Your practice is the mindful interaction with the spirit of and in life and yourself. It is an opportunity to affirm the moment and your conscious participation in life. It is a conscious choice to open the door to experience the Oneness in yourself and the spirit that moves in all things.

Your daily spiritual practice is a gift that you give to yourself. It is an opportunity to mindfully unify your body, mind, and spirit by bringing things into balance, inviting healing, "working" on yourself, moving personal energy, and connecting with life-force energies. The personal healing techniques, journeys, and exercises presented in the previous chapters are your tickets to the unification, healing, and shamanic living you seek.

Through the focused intention of your practice, you can connect with these energies for the time that you are in practice, and you can bring them into your everyday life as well. Want to keep your soul connected, emotions calm, thoughts clear, and body healthy? Looking to find the calm and peace of solitude in your life, or heal from an imbalance such as fatigue, depression, pain, or illness? Take a journey, do a ceremony, meditate, go for a shamanic walk, and see what happens for you. Drifting away to the sound of the drumbeat or talking to the trees for just fifteen minutes a day will go a long way in unifying body, mind, and soul, and linking you to the vital energies of the Web. It is easy, but requires focus and discipline. You must make yourself a priority.

Some people find it difficult to give themselves time for a spiritual practice, but find it easier to give themselves time for a life-giving practice. The difference? Perception. Taking time out of an already busy schedule for spiritual purposes often ends up getting justified out the door. "I have this to do and that to do, so I'll journey tomorrow." Thinking of your practice as a life-giving practice may change it from a "have to" to a "want to." By engaging in a daily practice and consciously choosing to be aware throughout the day, you are giving yourself the energy and power to live life with gusto. Have you seen a child run around just for the pure joy of running? That's the power and energy this practice can give you. We recommend that you give yourself an hour of power per day.

Now, before you say, "No way!" take a deep breath and relax. We don't mean an hour all at once, if that doesn't work for you. We mean an hour, total, throughout the day, when you are consciously choosing to connect mind, body, soul, personal medicine wheel, helping spirits, and Otherworld energies. For some, this hour is a combination of journey in the morning and prayer at night. For some, it is a brisk shaman's walk (exercise three in this chapter) in the morning and a quiet, simple ceremony of gratitude in the evening. For some, it is an extraction, soul retrieval, or recapitulation-and-reclamation journey for an hour on a day off. For another, it is a short journey at lunch, several brief breaks of deep breathing, and an overall dedication to being aware by checking Within to notice what is being thought, felt, sensed, and experienced throughout the day. For another, it is conscious love-making followed by a journey or "staring off into space" to integrate energies. Another might view this time as an opportune time to "hollow the bone" or clear the channels by doing any of the techniques, journeys, and exercises recommended. Someone else might find it helpful to focus on and embody their Earth connection by tapping into the energetic umbilical cord that runs through the spinal column into the Earth, appearing as a golden cord of connection to some. Don't believe any of these suggestions? Just do it and see what happens for you. Your spiritual practice must be of your own creation. You know what feels helpful and works best for you. If not, experiment. You are your own shaman. You are the captain of your own ship. There is no wrong way to do your spiritual practice.

Everyday Life

Shamanism isn't a religion or merely a spiritual practice—it's a way of being and living. What we *do* with and within ourselves is what we *do* in the world. Your everyday life is an expression of what is really going on with you. You might be expressing your soul, or you might be expressing your issues. Living shamanically means knowing the difference and choosing to live from the soul as much as possible. To do so, you will want to be aware of your issues and programs not only in your spiritual practice, but also in your everyday life. By paying attention to the things that happen in your life, you will receive the messages that you need in order to do your inner work. Notice what you are thinking, feeling, doing, saying, how you are behaving, and why. Explore and investigate your psyche, realizing that your thoughts and feelings are really only your way of looking at things. Are you living from your united soul, mind, and body, or is there an issue going on that causes you to be off balance or to express a program? Self-awareness helps you see the difference. Notice what is happening around you; what you see, sense, and feel; and what others are saying and doing. All communication carries a message for you, and all interactions are mirrors with which you can see yourself.

Your everyday, ordinary life and everything in it is just as sacred as your altar and daily spiritual practice. How could it not be when everything is a soul and everything is energy? The reason that most folks don't see everyday life as sacred is, again, based on that old belief that things are separate. They aren't. Living mindfully, aware of the sacred in all things, could profoundly change your life. Perhaps this story will help illustrate.

Colleen's grandmother used to talk to the dishes. She would stand at the sink, eyes glazed and head cocked to the side, lovingly cleaning the crockery with caresses from her washrag. She would whisper very softly, then listen intently, then speak again. Sometimes she would laugh, sometimes softly murmur an affirmative mm-hmm or uh-huh or a nodding yes. The dishes were talking back, and they were telling her things she needed or wanted to know. She often received funny looks from folks at church when she told them her dishwashing stories, but she loved her work and saw the life in all things. Talking dishes—now that is animism! She lived in vibrant health to nearly ninety-four years of age. Maybe there is something to animism, huh? We suggest communicating as if all things are souls. Talk to the trees, feel the energy of the seasons, and sense the moon cycles. Be a part of it all, rather than a separate being.

We shamans are hunters and gatherers of energy that we use to make a difference in our selves, lives, and world. In addition to harnessing energy, we must pay attention to where and how we use our energy. Again, self-awareness is the key. Take notice throughout the day. Where is your energy? How do you feel energetically? What are you doing, thinking, and feeling? How does your body feel? Is it sending you any messages through fatigue, pain, or discomfort? Are you experiencing any imbalances that you can affect right now with a short journey or energy-connecting exercise? Where is your emotional, mental, physical, and spiritual energy going, and what is it doing? It is important to realize that what you give energy to, you give life to. Check in often to see what you are giving life to.

One of the most obvious hidden-in-plain-sight examples of this statement is reality. What we believe to be real, we consciously and unconsciously give energy to, and thus we create our reality. Once you embrace this idea, you will find it imperative to know what you believe, what you believe to be real, and what you value. Everything in your inner and outer world revolves around what you believe. If you believe that you are unlovable, you will have relationship issues. If you believe that you don't deserve health or abundance, you will have health and financial struggles. If you believe that you are a charmed, loved, healthy person, you will be. We suggest you spend some time exploring your beliefs. You might be surprised what you find.

Another place where energy is often spent unconsciously is in the boundary areas of stance. Your stance is an inner knowing of what you stand for, what is truly real and vitally important to you, and what you would lay your life on the line for. Find it, but don't grasp it. Your stance isn't something you hold on to; it's something you just know inside and stand on as a foundation. Be as fluid, flexible, and unattached as you can to what you stand for. It seems contradictory, but what you stand on can also trap you if don't stay open to new information coming in. Knowing yourself and your stance, while keeping your eyes wide open and being willing to try on new or different points of view, is a powerful way to live. Try it. Try seeing the world from the point of view of your neighbor, your coworker, a tree, a rock, a moose, or a star. We think you'll find that this way of seeing is much broader than your own narrow point of view and helps you stay open to learning and seeing a whole lot more.

Truth is another place where most of us unconsciously tie up energy. Unfortunately, we are very rarely completely truthful, even when we think we are. We live in a culture where white lies are expected and big lies are easily justified by such things as our feelings or the actions of another. The truth of the matter is, we are all lying the biggest lie of all: the lie to ourselves. One of our teachers says that lying is a global program. If a person is willing to lie to their spouse, their boss, or the IRS, they will certainly be willing to lie to themselves. The solution to this problem is a simple one. We must often ask ourselves if we are telling ourselves the truth and honestly listen to the answer using our truth spot. This simple question—am I telling the truth, or am I lying to myself?—can free up an enormous amount of personal energy. This is a question shamans ask themselves in every conversation in the ordinary world and in their daily spiritual practice.

Graham Greene once said, "When we are not sure, we are alive." Shamans are students of life. Everything and everyone is our teacher. Be aware, awake, alert, and observant both externally and internally. Watch and listen without interpretation or judgment. When you are able to watch without analysis, you will notice a natural flow, a natural order of how things "work" when there is no intervention or interference. Likewise, you will begin to notice when things feel forced, out of balance, or manipulated in some way. Shamans make these observations and learn about life, people, and energy from them.

Your job, as shaman and student of life, is to notice the countless, diverse ways that Spirit attempts to communicate with you all the time. Signs in nature, the things that people say, songs of personal significance that synchronistically come on the radio or that have messages in the lyrics, or even something as seemingly random as images on the truck you are passing—these all are messages from your soul and the helping spirits to your conscious awareness. *Omenology* is the name given to this technique of awareness. By paying attention to everything that happens around us, we become aware of the internal and universal messages and signposts that mark our paths through life. These messages are available everywhere within ourselves and our world when we look, listen, feel, and acknowledge. If we then use our skills of intuition to let those occurrences sit within us, they will give us insight and guidance. Pay attention to these signs. They will likely have great meaning for you, guide you in a certain direction, or help you make sense of something you are trying to learn.

Energy is lost any time that we are living from the mind rather than the unification of mind, body, and soul. One of the ways we lose energy is when we live according to our obligations instead of our choices. We have been trained well to live as others think we should live rather than how we would choose to live. You can free

up enormous amounts of personal energy by choosing to deliber-
ately live the life you want—not the life your ego wants, but the life
that your soul wants.

So what is the life your soul wants? Well, a life where the soul is
free to express itself, that's what. Do your inner work to clear out
the blockages and programs, and your soul will have a clear pathway for expression in your life and in the world. Explore and find
out what your soul path is, and then honor that path. Shine brightly
out into the world and keep doing your healing, program releasing,
and ego-dismantling work every day. Keep growing and evolving.
Keep learning. Be at peace with yourself. If you are not, find out
why. Explore yourself, and ask others to share their observations
honestly.

You are your own shaman, but you shouldn't operate in a vacuum.
We encourage you to create a community that supports your choice
to live shamanically. Observe and learn from others, ask your friends
and family to share their points of view and to be mirrors for you,
and share your discoveries with them. Perhaps you will feel drawn to
develop a shamanic community—a group dedicated to such things
as talking, reading books, discussing, mirroring for one another, rewriting programs, soul healing, drumming, rattling, dancing, singing, journeying, ceremony, ritual, community service, and sharing
experiences. .

Individually or collectively in your group, you would benefit from
and enjoy giving back to the world. Some of our best personal-growth
lessons can come from doing something to make a difference for
someone else. When we step outside of ourselves and become less
self-focused and attached to our own lives, thoughts, viewpoints,
opinions, and feelings, we can begin to see what is happening for
other people and in the world. This view, in turn, helps us more easily see the bigger picture of our own lives. Step outside your separate life with open eyes, see the beauty, feel the pain, and you will
find that we really are all one tribe and always have been, in this age
and the age to come.

Journeys

State your intention to journey to any of the three worlds (unless specified), meet with your helping spirits, and do the following:

- Journey to the message of the song at the beginning of the chapter. Explore what this message means to and for you.

- Explore the concept of Oneness. What do the helping spirits have to teach you about this concept?

- Ask to be shown how you can unify body, mind, and soul.

- Ask to be shown where you are needlessly spending energy in your everyday life.

- Ask to be shown where and how you can garner energy in your daily practice and everyday life.

- Ask how you can develop a daily life-giving practice that would be beneficial to you.

- Ask how to develop your bare awareness in everyday life.

- Explore, learn about, and ask to be shown the sacred in all things.

- Journey to your personal medicine wheel for energy, wisdom, learning, power, and medicine.

- Ask to be taken to your Otherworld home. Notice what your home looks and feels like. Notice who and what is there. Notice your luminous energy body. Does your Otherworld home symbolize your soul-self, body, or energy field? Tidy up your home if you need to. Relight fires, sweep out cobwebs and dust, and so on.

- Ask about the usable power in your Otherworld home. What does it look like and feel like? What does it do to your energy body? How can you connect with it and use it in your everyday life? Walk outside, open your mind, and have an adventure of power. Go on a power quest!

- Return to your Otherworld home. Inside or nearby you will find a treasure chest. Don't look in. Instead, reach in and pull out three different items. What do they mean to you? Ask for clarity on the items, and ask what agreements or aspects need to be accepted or released in order for you to utilize these items. Hold the items and feel the energy.

- Return to your Otherworld home. Walk out in back of it to a pond. Look in and ask to see your spiritual-warrior aspect or your soul-self. Merge with your spiritual-warrior self or your soul-self.

- Ask to be shown how the spirits are speaking to you through omens.

- Journey to learn about natural order. Release your point of view, your judgments, and what you think you know. Ask what natural order is.

- Observe nature through the eyes of your helping spirits and ask to be shown the natural order in nature.

- Ask what interferes with natural order. Do judgments, dichotomies, programs, personal will, stubborn opinions, ego, or even a desire to help interfere with it?

- Ask to be shown where you have lost natural order in your life. When, why, how did you lose it? Don't do anything to change it. Use this opportunity to explore and learn.

- Ask to be shown how natural order or the lack thereof affects relationships and agreements. What does natural order mean for and to you in your relationships and agreements?

- Ask what will, or how you can, restore the natural order of your life.

- Explore the idea that you create your own reality. What does this idea mean to and for you? Ask to be shown how you create your own reality. Are there things that you need to change? Are there things that you need to implement?

- Ask to be shown what you need to know and do to be a student of life.
- Ask how to build a spiritual or mindful community.
- Ask how you can help make a difference with others and in the world.

Exercises

Exercise One: Pledge to the Spirits

Pledging and commitment ceremonies have many different variations. The one described here was gifted to us in a workshop by renowned Celtic shaman, author, and teacher Tom Cowan.

A pledge to the spirits is a significant act that should not be taken lightly. It is a powerful way to make a statement about something that you want to dedicate yourself to. In this commitment to the spirits, yourself, the elements, and powers of the universe, you make a binding agreement to do what you pledge. Because of this contract, it is important to perform this ceremony only when you are ready and are serious about making your pledge.

Take great care when formulating your pledge. Words are power. Words and the way words are put together can have meanings beyond our present level of comprehension. So use words that are specific and that clearly state what you want to say. Avoid words that have nebulous or double meanings. Always state your pledge as if it is already happening. Avoid "later-elsewhere" phrases such as "I will," "I want to," or "when needed." Instead, formulate your pledge around the words "I do" or "I am." Because wording is so important, it is good practice to journey to consult with the spirits, making sure you are asking for what is truly desired for your highest good.

When you have formulated your pledge, write it down on a piece of cloth and tear the cloth in half. Put one half of the cloth in a place of honor where you will see it, such as on your altar or on a shamanic tool. Take the other half of the cloth to a sacred outdoor location of

your choice. Invite your helping spirits to join you and drum, rattle, sing, dance, chant, or pray to build power. When the power is
strong, hold the cloth up to the sky and the spirits and, with resolve,
speak your pledge out loud three times. Immediately pay attention
to your surroundings and take note of the first three things that you
hear or see. These will be omens or signs that will help you remember and honor your pledge. Tie your cloth to something at the site,
such as a tree, and leave it there for the spirits and the elements to
caress, activate, and witness through the years. Use your felt sense
and notice what you are experiencing.

When you are finished, thank your helping spirits and tell them
the work is done for now. Relax and take a few moments to journal
your experience before leaving this sacred place.

Exercise Two: Divination

There are an infinite number of ways to seek insight and guidance.
One simple, practical method is to use a deck of oracle cards that
appeals to you. Any deck will do.

Once you have your cards, make yourself comfortable in your
soft space. Inhale and exhale a few deep breaths, and relax your
body and mind. Drum or rattle for a few minutes to shift your consciousness, and relax deeper. When you feel sufficiently calm and
relaxed, take a few minutes to form the question that you would like
to ask. Words have power, so be sure to take your time and ask the
exact question that you are seeking guidance for.

When the question is formed, spread the cards out in front of you
and ask the question. Use your felt sense to feel and sense which
card will give you the insight you need most at this time. Draw the
card. Observe how you feel upon seeing it. Notice the pictures, messages, artwork, and symbols on the card. What do they mean to you?
Read the description of the card in the accompanying booklet, if there
is one. Notice your thoughts and feelings. What does the card mean
to you? Journal your experience. As you go about your daily life, pay

attention to any omens or signs that may add additional insights to this exercise.

Exercise Three: Omenology Awareness/Shaman's Walk

A shaman's walk is an exercise in awareness and omenology. The components are a question, a walk, and bare awareness, your felt sense, and intuition. Inhale, and exhale a few deep breaths, and begin to relax your body and mind. Drum or rattle for a few minutes to shift your consciousness, and relax deeper. Form the question that you would like to ask, remembering that words have power. When the question is formed, speak the question slowly out loud three times as you begin your walk and again periodically throughout your walk. Pay attention to anything and everything that you see, feel, sense, and experience while on your walk. Notice the messages all around and within you. What do these messages mean to and for you? Journal your experience. As you go about your daily life, pay attention to any omens or signs that may add additional insights.

Exercise Four: Oneness

This exercise will help you experience the unity of yourself and the Oneness of all things. To begin, put on a CD of drumming or trance-inducing music. Stand in a comfortable position, with your arms down at your sides. One by one, notice your body, then your thoughts, then your feelings and emotions. Notice how you feel all over, inside and out.

Now let everything drop away as you dance to the rhythm. Lose your body, emotions, and mind. Dance like a bag of bones, like a skeleton moving to the beat. Completely lose yourself and become a raindrop dancing down from the sky into the vast ocean. You are the ocean, and then you are the Web of Life, and then you are the whole universe, and then you are nothing but pure soul energy—a bright light shining out into the world.

The future world may or may not be much like the world we are living in now. No one has any way of knowing. There may always be the good, the bad, the ugly, and the beautiful. Or there may not. That is out of our control and sight.

One thing we do know to be true is that the planet and her inhabitants, and therefore we and our world, are ever changing and evolving. Who and what will you be in that evolution? is the real question. What will you bring to the table in the coming age? What do you agree to make real? Where will you responsibly apply your awareness and energy to make a difference?

CLOSING PRAYER

As I Walk with Beauty
As I walk, as I walk
The universe is walking with me
In beauty it walks before me
In beauty it walks behind me
In beauty it walks below me
In beauty it walks above me
Beauty is on every side
As I walk, I walk with Beauty.

—Traditional Navajo prayer

Appendix:
Treatment Chart

Challenge	Probable Energetic Cause	Recommended Shamanic Methods
General	Aches and pains, Emotional and energetic blockages, yearning for connection, power loss	Energy cleansing, energy movement, extraction, disemberment, soul-self connection, connection with Spirit
Addictions	Emotional and energetic blockages, conflict between objective reality and personal beliefs and actions, programs, possession, intrusions	Energy movement, recapitulation and reclamation, energy cleansing, depossession/psychopomp, extraction
Anxiety (panic attacks, worry)	Emotional and energetic blockages, conflict between objective reality and personal beliefs and actions, programs	Energy movement, recapitulation and reclamation, energy cleansing
Burnout or world-weariness	Emotional and energetic blockages, stagnant energy, programs, energy leakage	Energy cleansing, energy movement, recapitulation and reclamation, energy-boundary fortification
Depression	Power loss, dispiritedness, soul loss, soul-self disconnection, conflict between objective reality and personal beliefs and actions, programs, intrusions, possession	Power retrieval, soul retrieval, recapitulation and reclamation, extraction, depossession/psychopomp
Dissatisfaction	Soul-self or soul-path disconnection, programs	Soul-self or soul-path reconnection, recapitulation and reclamation

Appendix:
Treatment Chart
(continued)

Challenge	Probable Energetic Cause	Recommended Shamanic Methods
Emptiness	Dispiritedness, soul-self disconnection, soul loss	Connection with Spirit, soul-self reconnection, soul retrieval, power-filling
Fatigue/low energy	Power loss, dispiritedness, stagnant energy, energy leakage	Connection with Spirit, energy movement, energy-boundary fortification, cord cutting
Physical illness and injury, Acute, localized pain/discomfort	Intrusions, blockages, energy leakages	Extraction, energy movement, energy clearing, energy boundary
Physical illness and injury, Chronic	Power loss, dispirited, soul loss, energy blockages	Connect with Spirit, soul retrieval, extraction, dismemberment, energy movement, power filling
Stress/tension	Energy blockages, programs	Power filling, energy movement, recapitulation and reclamation

Endnotes

i Tom Cowan, workshop handout, *www.riverdrum.com*.

ii Michael Harner, The Way of the Shaman, 3rd ed. (San Francisco: HarperSan Francisco, 1990).

iii John Worthington, *The Office of Shaman*, The Other Connection, 2007. Available online at *www.theotherforum.net*.

iv Victor Sanchez, Presentation at the International Conference on Shamanism. Available through The Message Company, Santa Fe, NM, 2006.

v James David Audlin, *Circle of Life* (Santa Fe, NM: Clear Light Books, 2004), p. 208.

vi Mark Stavish, *The Path of Alchemy: Energetic Healing and the World of Natural Magic* (St. Paul, MN: Llewellyn Publications, 2006).

vii Ted Andrews, *Animal-Speak: The Spiritual & Magical Powers of Creatures Great & Small* (St. Paul, MN: Llewellyn Publications, 1996), p. 9.

viii Colleen Deatsman, *Energy for Life: Connect with the Source* (St. Paul, MN: Llewellyn Publications, 2006).

ix Sandra Ingerman, *Soul Retrieval: Mending the Fragmented Self* (San Francisco, CA: HarperSanFrancisco, 1991), p. 1.

x Colleen Deatsman, *Inner Power: Six Techniques for Increased Energy and Self-Healing* (St. Paul, MN: Llewellyn Publications, 2005).

xi Barb Barton, "Circles," *From the Eye of Hawk*, 1993. Available at *www.barbbarton.com*.

xii Roger Highfield, "Surfer dude stuns physicists with theory of everything," *Telegraph.co.uk*, November 14, 2007. *http://www.telegraph.co.uk/earth/main.jhtml?view=DETAILS&grid=&xml=/earth/2007/11/14/scisurf114.xml* (04/22/08).

ABOUT THE AUTHORS

Colleen Deatsman has been exploring health and wellness, self-healing, personal growth, and spiritual development for over 25 years. She is a Licensed Professional Counselor, Licensed Social Worker, Usui Reiki Master, Certified Clinical Hypnotherapist, Certified Alternative Healing Consultant, Shamanic Practitioner, and author of three previous books. For ten years, Colleen dealt with the effects of a chronic illness that traditional medicine could not effectively treat. Determined to live life fully again, she embarked on a journey of self-healing that eventually led to complete recovery and a comprehensive new program that she now teaches in workshops and classes. She lives in Mason, MI. For information about "The Deatsman Program" trainings, as well as her online classes in shamanism, see *www.colleendeatsman.com*.

Paul Bowersox is a shamanic teacher and practitioner, writing coach, editor, and contributing writer for a number of publications and authors. He has studied extensively with shamanism experts Michael Harner, Sandra Ingerman, Tom Cowan, Larry Peters, John Worthington, David Corbin, and Nan Moss. He lives in Bloomsburg, PA.